How To Make & Sell Quality *Teddy Bears*

By Terry & Doris Michaud

Photography by Thomas J. Mocny

Published by **Hobby House Press** Grantsville, Maryland 21536

Additional copies of this book may be purchased at $12.95
from
Hobby House Press, Inc.
1 Corporate Drive
Grantsville, Maryland 21536
1-800-554-1447
(please add $4.75 per copy for postage)
or from your favorite bookstore or dealer.

©1986 Terry and Doris Michaud
Second Printing January 1991
Third Printing January 1994
Fourth Printing January 1996

ISBN: 0-87588-416-4

Table of Contents

Dedication

This book is dedicated to Teddy Bear collectors world wide, the most sophisticated, dedicated, caring and sharing people it has been our pleasure to meet. It is for you the artist strives to create and to perfect. Without you, our work is insignificant.

Acknowledgements

We wish to thank the many kind people who shared their experiences to make this book possible. Among them are: Stuarte Browne of Monterey Mills, Robert Hall of Norton Weaving Ltd. in England, Madeline Daddiego of the Mohair Council of America, Mickie Veale of Creekwood Bear Co., Donna Harrison and Dottie Ayers of Calico Teddy, Jane Servinski of Maple Hill Nursery and Doll Shoppe, Beth Savino of Hobby Center Toys stores, Joan Venturino of Bears To Go, our Teddy Bear artist friends whose contributions were immensely helpful including Beverly Port, Mary Olsen, Sharon July, Elaine Fujita-Gamble, Dickie Harrison and Sara Phillips, and the collectors whose input was most important including Susan Allis, Marilyn M. Risch, Sig and Sandy Humanski, Margaret J. Lee, Jack McCutchan and Paul and Rosemary Volpp. It is impossible to undertake a project of this scope without overlooking someone. To that person, we apologize.

Our foremost gratitude has to go to our photographer Thomas J. Mocny, Editor Donna H. Felger and Publisher Gary R. Ruddell who provided us the means of sharing.

Foreword

Whether you want to create the delightful jointed Teddy Bear on the cover for your very own collection, or you want to embark on a career of producing Teddy Bears for collectors the world over, this book is for you! Within you will find a Teddy Bear project, with complete pattern and detailed instructions on construction. We will also show you how you can produce dramatically different Teddies from the same pattern just by choice of fabric and other variations.

One section is devoted to the discussion of fabrics, from modacrylics to mohair, and how to choose the right plush for your project. There is a thorough discussion of all bear-making supplies, including the Carrousel riveted joint system.

An important section for the budding artist is the chapter on designing Teddy Bears. We will show you how to create your own pattern and how to make slight modifications to produce the desired result. This section will include some guidelines on how to obtain a copyright for your work.

In the Marketing section, this book goes into an in-depth discussion on what to do with Teddy once he is completed (assuming you are willing to part with him!). You will find guidelines on where and how to sell your bear, and most importantly, how to determine a fair market price. This section will be of value whether you are part of a fund-raising group or an entrepreneur with a goal of creating an exciting business.

The guidelines and factual information presented here are not limited to the Teddy Bear maker, but can be a valuable resource to the crafts person who sells or wants to sell at craft sales, church bazaars or in the commercial marketplace. We have tried to share not only our experience in building our highly successful Carrousel business, but we have received input from many friends and business associates who have taken time to share their expertise.

The path to your completed project or goal may be strewn with frustrations and disappointment, but the joy of creating something that brings pleasure and happiness to others more than compensates for the effort. It is our sincere hope that this book will light a creative fire in you that will burn brightly for the rest of your days.

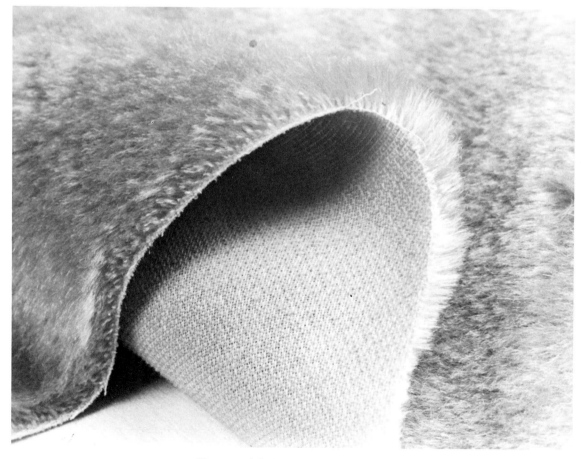

Choose a fabric with a dense pile.

Poor quality mohair shows much of the backing. Note dense mohair sample in background.

Hold that pose!

Designing Teddy Bears is tedious but challenging.

Carrousel Teddy Bears.
Back row left: *Sir Edward III, 27in (69cm).*
Right: *Sir Edward II, 18in (46cm).* **Front:** *Baby Edward, 13in (33cm). All acrylic plush.*

Carrousel's Burnt Umbear, 18in (46cm), in acrylic plush, sketching his old friend, The Professor.

Brother Theodore by Carrousel in acrylic plush, 18in (46cm), leading Donkey by Gebrüder Hermann.

Danny Boy by Carrousel, 18in (46cm), contains Reuge Swiss music box that plays Danny Boy. Acrylic plush.

Johann in acrylic plush stands 18in (46cm), with Reuge Swiss music box that plays Edelweiss. Leather lederhosen by Tailormaid Togs. Bear by Carrousel.

Ted the Good News Bear'r by Carrousel, 18in (46cm), discovers a friend. Dog by Sandicast.

Bearzo the Clown by Carrousel, 18in (46cm), takes a ride astride goose by Velvet Stable. Bearzo is acrylic plush.

Left: *original Just Ted, 18in (46cm), circa 1924.* **Right:** *Just Ted recreation by Carrousel in acrylic plush, 18in (46cm). Croquet set circa 1910.*

Left: original Professor, 18in (46cm), circa 1915. *Right:* Carrousel's recreation of The Professor in mohair blend, 18in (46cm).

Left: original Eddie, 15in (38cm), circa 1904. *RIGHT:* Carrousel recreation in mohair blend, 15in (38cm). Diecast model cars by Solido.

Becky Mae, a Stearnsy Bear by Teddy Bear artists Jim and Sally Stearns. 11in (28cm). Acrylic plush.

Four very different Teddies, all made from the pattern in this book. **Front, left to right:** *mohair blend, wool cashmere blend, 80-year-old quilt.* **Back row:** *acrylic plush. All Teddies stand 11in (28cm).*

Add a bow and he's ready to go!   *Mohair Teddy from book pattern.*

A plaid muffler turns Teddy into a Scotsman.

A leather dog collar gives Teddy a different look.

A salesman's sample hat and he is most distinguished.

Antique wire rim glasses, a straw hat and bow tie and our friend looks like Harold Lloyd, a motion picture comic from the 1920s.

The Cashmere Teddy awaits his wardrobe.

Or, he can be a sailor girl in an outfit borrowed from the doll clothing rack.

The patchwork quilt bear has loads of character by himself.

A starched collar from an antique shop adds a touch of charm.

A lace shawl is an appropriate touch in keeping with Teddy's quilt age.

Our acrylic plush version needs something from the closet.

A stocking hat and green bow give him a Christmas touch.

Pantaloons, bathing cap and umbrella and we're ready for the beach.

A knitted sweater can be worn to the front or back.

ABOVE: *The bear making process starts with material selection (our choice is mohair blend).*

RIGHT: *Each pattern piece is pinned and cut.*

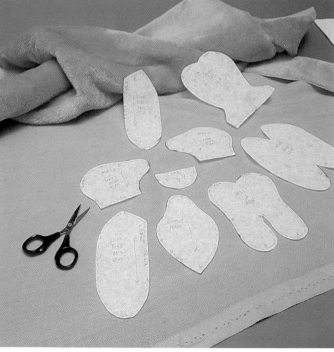

18

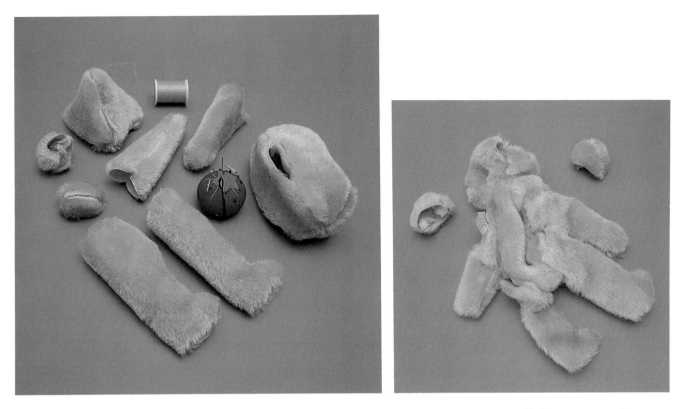

Parts are machine sewn.

Joints are installed, eyes are put in.

Boy, am I stuffed!

First phase of finishing includes hand sewing openings, sewing ears in place.

With muzzle shaved, nose and mouth are finished and Teddy is so pleased he does cartwheels.

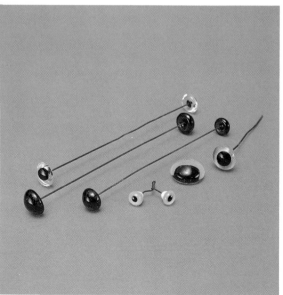

Glass eyes used in taxidermy are well suited for Teddy Bears.

ABOVE: *Plastic eyes come in many sizes and colors.*

RIGHT: *Doris and Terry Michaud on their gingerbread porch with the four unique bears made from one pattern.*

BELOW: *The Carrousel Shop and Museum is located in a beautiful Victorian mansion built in 1895.*

Dickie Harrison's miniature version of The Professor!

A miniature Panda and Carrousel Bear made for the Michauds by Sara Phillips.

A delightful miniature by Elaine Fujita-Gamble.

Debonair Bear by Sara Phillips.

A hand-carved wooden Teddy.

A miniature Yes/No bear by Dickie Harrison.

A tiny ceramic pin cushion bear.

The latest Carrousel recreation from their Museum collection is based on this 1904 original. Eddie is 15in (38cm) and was given to a boy named Eddie by a neighbor girl who grew up to fame and fortune as Marilyn Miller of Ziegfield Follies fame.

Chapter One:
The Carrousel Story

When discussing the Carrousel story in lectures, we frequently make reference to our business as "a hobby that got carried away." There is more than a small measure of truth to this. Our combined backgrounds in the sales and technical engineering fields have made very strong contributions, but our business and creative skills were greatly enhanced by a hobby that started in 1967.

We received an antique wall clock from someone in our family, and it sparked an interest in other antiques as well. We joined friends who frequented antique auctions and ended up with more than our share of treasures from yesteryear. In order to support our new-found hobby, it became necessary to sell a few of the things that we acquired. We found that if we bought an item that needed a modest amount of repair, we could restore it and then sell the item for enough profit to buy two more. We became so proficient at stripping and refinishing furniture that we joined forces with a relative to open a furniture stripping shop. Business was always brisk, due in great part to the fact that very few people enjoy this somewhat messy job. In fact, it became a problem for two families to keep up with the volume of business generated, since neither of us were in a position to make it a full time occupation. So, the business was sold.

We started to explore other avenues that would allow us to continue with our antiques business but not be so demanding on our time. Antique shows held in shopping malls were just coming into popularity, and we examined the potential of going this route. It had a number of things going for it that attracted us. We could do shows and not have to maintain daily shop hours. We could travel a small geographic area and expand our potential customer base. Perhaps the most attractive factor was the reasonable cost to do these shows, given the large volume exposure to collectors. After scouting out a few shows in our area, we booked our first mall show. By now we had decided that most shows had more than a fair number of furniture and glassware dealers, so we decided to specialize in old toys and dolls.

Since this endeavor did not represent a full time occupation, we were able to put back all the profits generated into the business and as a result, we experienced a rapid growth. It was tempting to set aside some of the more unusual and desirable pieces to start our own collection, but if we kept every piece that we were attracted to, we would soon be out of business! We, therefore, made a pact that all pieces acquired would be for sale. On occasion we would come across an item that we would price high enough to discourage someone from buying it, but even that does not always work.

Since our specialty focused on children's things, we added shows to our schedule that were devoted exclusively to antique and collectible dolls and toys. It meant that we would have to travel greater distances for the shows, but it was well worth the effort since it put us in contact with a much greater concentration of toy and doll collectors. We had built up a following of doll collectors but at this point in time Teddy Bear collectors were few and far between. An occasional doll collector would admit to liking the furry little creatures and so every now and then a Teddy Bear would pass through our hands to a small group of interested people.

In 1972, we were attending an antique doll show in Holt, a suburb of Lansing, Michigan. There we were to acquire The Professor, a Teddy Bear that was to turn our lives upside down. Making the rounds of the other dealers set up at the show, we came upon a table with the usual assortment of collectible dolls. The dealer was only partially set up, still unpacking cardboard boxes sitting around her on the floor. There, lying half upside down in one of the boxes, was a well-worn mohair Teddy from the 1915 era. Closer examination revealed this bedraggled bear had but one ear. Since doll repair had been added to our stable of services, it would be an easy matter to make him right.

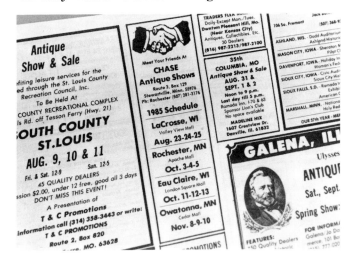

Antique shows are a great place to find old Teddy Bears.

Playthings of yesterday.

"How much for the old worn bear?" Terry inquired.

"Twenty dollars," the dealer responded.

"I'm a dealer and I'll go fifteen," Terry answered.

"Oh, I guess there's not much interest in Teddy Bears so you've got a deal," replied the dealer, dropping the bear in a bag.

The normal procedure would have been to place Teddy in the overflowing box of dolls and toys needing repair, but there was something about this Teddy that demanded immediate attention. Doris removed the good ear and opened the center seam on it, creating two old fronts. Backing each with a similar material restored the bear to his original appearance. A doll sweater was unearthed from the goodie box where such things are stored, and a pair of antique eyeglasses were added, now that Teddy had the two ears necessary to wear glasses.

As we sat back to admire the obvious captivating charm our new found friend exhibited, our daughter entered the room and exclaimed, "Oh, my gosh! He looks just like my music teacher. He even has cat hair and dandruff on his sweater!"

Remember that cardinal rule we had about selling everything that passed through our hands? It was about to be violated. We decided that if we kept this Teddy (who had acquired the name "The Professor"), we could stand him in our booth at shows, holding a sign saying "Wanted — Old Teddy Bears." The bear and the sign worked their magic at the shows that were to follow, and the collection rapidly grew into an addiction. There was never a conscientious decision to collect Teddy Bears; it was just that the thought of selling one simply never entered our minds after that.

Many times during the ensuing years we would question our sanity in spending a hundred dollars or more for an early German Teddy Bear in excellent condition. It would be nice to believe that we had the

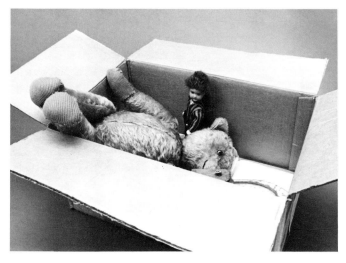

"How much for the old bear in the box?"

foresight to recognize not only the excellent investment, but to realize what an important role this collection would eventually play in our business. It is probably more accurate to say that when The Professor entered our lives, we simply grabbed onto the back of his sweater as he led us down the path, just as he continues to lead the way today.

With the low level of interest in Teddy Bears by collectors and our frequent opportunity to uncover them at doll and toy shows, our collection grew at an astonishing rate. The late Peter Bull's books in the late sixties and early seventies led us into a new era for Teddy Bear collectors that has not yet peaked.

While we were primarily interested in Teddy Bears 40 years and older, we kept abreast of the contemporary market and would, on occasion, add a new Teddy to the collection. During a visit to Boston I had the opportunity of discussing the Teddy Bear market with a shop owner. I asked if he knew of any company in the United States that produced a Teddy Bear that had all of the characteristics of the antique Teddies, with movable joints, glass eyes and hump back. He said that he had been looking for just such a company but had been unable to find one. I assured him that someone was going to make such a Teddy and filed his calling card into my pocket, feeling confident that I would be in touch within a month or so.

That "month or so" turned into two years before we were able to produce a Teddy Bear that met our standards. Our first approach was to work with commercial patterns. While the Teddies had a certain measure of charm and appeal, they simply did not have that special characteristic we were looking for. We then followed an old adage Terry had learned as an engineer, that is to "never let common sense stand in the way of a good project." If you think you cannot do something, you are probably right. But if you assume it is simply a question of knowing you can, but finding the right way, you are well on the road to success.

Let us not leave you with the impression that the two-year development period was by any means easy. Terry would lay out a proposed design, cut out the pattern and hand it over for sewing. Before it was half assembled, he would proclaim it was not what he had in mind after all and go back to the drawing board. We reached a point where a firm suggestion was made to "hire a seamstress if you don't like the way I do it!" Terry did just that but the results were still not forthcoming, and worst of all, they had to be paid for their work, regardless of results.

A truce was called and we sat down to analyze where we were and where we wanted to get. We examined a dozen or so of our favorite Teddy Bears from the collection to see if we could specifically pinpoint what the special attraction was in each. Somehow these features seemed to fit together into

The Professor at work.

one single design and we were at last able to produce a Teddy Bear that met our mind's eye view of what he should look like.

During the course of this design effort, we had begun to correspond with Peter Bull. We completed a successful prototype just about the time we decided to make a Teddy Bear hunting excursion to England. We felt it appropriate to take one of our first Teddies along as a gift to the man who had enriched the lives of so many Teddy Bear collectors. Peter was every bit as warm and friendly as we anticipated he would be and more than generous in his praise of our Teddy Bear design. He encouraged us to begin producing them, and shortly after our return we sent Sir Edward II to the Bear Necessities in Boston. Two very special friends, Edward and Rosemary Bastow, had accompanied us on a previous trip to England, so one of our very first Teddies went to them, dubbed Sir Edward. This meant that the first commercial model had to be Sir Edward II.

Shortly after Sir Edward II arrived in Boston, a phone call was received with an order placed for more Teddies of the same design. Carrousel Antiques became just Carrousel, and foot labels with our name and location were sewn into each bear. A toy dealer visiting Boston called and inquired about handling the bears in his store in another state. Teddy Bear fever was starting to spread from coast to coast and demand for our product spread just as rapidly. It is a simple matter of fact that we grew from that one shop to our present level of having our product in over 100 shops in 37 states without once asking a shop to handle them. While that statement rules out a brilliant marketing strategy, it does say something for producing a quality product at a fair price.

What began as a simple hobby has blossomed into a full time occupation that not only keeps us going from morning til night seven days a week, but commands the effort of eight to ten part-time helpers, including two daughters who assist us with much of the finish work. We were approached some time ago to take our design to a foreign producer who could dramatically reduce our labor costs. It was, of course, out of the question for it no longer would be "our" product. Accepting this limitation means we have to deal with a waiting list for new accounts since our production capability is limited, and we have to work with up to 90 day delivery schedules. However, we feel that every Carrousel Teddy Bear we produce carries a big part of us with it. That is why we are so richly rewarded when we receive a letter from a collector who tells us that her new Carrousel Teddy has stolen her heart and is her absolute favorite in her entire collection.

If you have picked this path for financial riches, you might be well advised to look elsewhere. But if you are motivated by a spark of creativity within that drives you to spend endless hours conceiving a finished product from cloth and thread that seems to possess a loving soul, then you are, by all means, on the right path.

This well-worn Teddy from the 30s acquired his old helmet from a doll and his "uniform" from a university gift shop.

The two books by the late Peter Bull that started the present day demand for Teddy Bears.

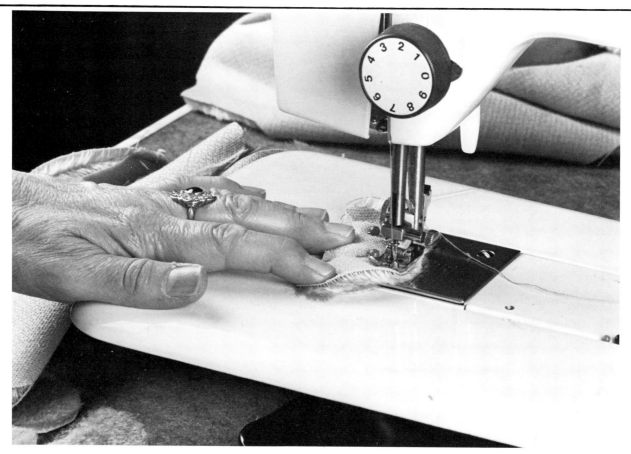

Design it, cut it, sew it. Then, start over again.

"If this one isn't right, he can just do the next one himself!"

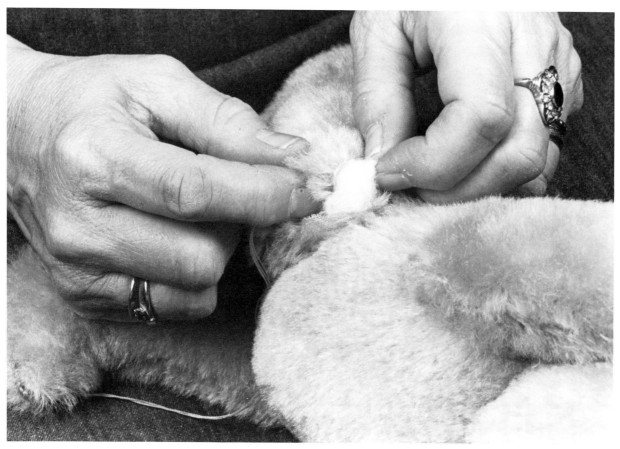

The very first Sir Edward II.

Every Carrousel Teddy wears a hang tag with The Professor's image on it.

Label your bear to identify and establish a reputation.

Terry and Doris' daughter, Mary Baese, is part of the family team.

Pat Messinger, a second daughter, is also actively engaged in the business.

Alison Gibson is an important member of the Carrousel team.

An early Carrousel Panda checks some mail from "home."

Chapter Two:
Teddy Bears Infinitus

Since their beginning in 1903, Teddy Bears have been made in an endless variety of materials. While our collection is primarily the typical plush variety, we include other Teddies, as well. We have a breathtaking pottery bear created by artists Frank and Suzy Bird of Texas, sitting astride a carrousel horse. We have ceramic and bisque bears, wood bears, a stunning cut glass crystal Teddy, and on occasion, we have had Teddy Bears made of ice cream and cookies (although they seem to disappear quickly!).

A typical "bag" bear (no moving joints).

A creation of artists Frank and Susie Bird.

Since most Teddy Bear collectors prefer the traditional plush design, we will limit our focus to this type. The early Teddy Bears were almost all fully-jointed, with movable heads, arms and legs. In the never-ending search by manufacturers to reduce prices, the "bag" bear came into being. This not only eliminated five joints, but reduced the number of parts and seams dramatically, thus reducing their expensive labor costs. Price became far more important than quality as producers competed for the children's toy market. Steiff and Hermann were two of the very small group of manufacturers who continued to emphasize quality and were, as a result, in the forefront when the adult collector market began to develop. Other Teddy Bear firms began to devote at least part of their production to an improved product, including a return to fully-jointed Teddies.

The ever growing collector's market gave birth to an entirely new category of craft person, the Teddy Bear artist. Handcrafted Teddy Bears can very likely be traced back to the very beginning. In fact, the early manufacturers actually employed a group of dedicated handcrafters who simply had no modern machinery to speed up production. It is also safe to assume that Teddy Bear artists (a hand-

A cut crystal Teddy with plenty of sparkle.

A terra cotta Teddy from England.

An old ceramic pincushion bear.

Doll artist John Wright's version of Winnie the Pooh.

crafter who works from his or her own pattern) were scattered here and there. But the actual categorizing of this skilled approach to Teddy Bear making is a more modern phenomenon. Beverly Port is an outstanding example of someone who has been involved with doll collecting and making for many years and evolved into a Teddy Bear artist with an enviable talent for creating Teddies that are coveted by collectors everywhere. Many of today's Teddy Bear artists and craft persons have come from the doll collecting hobby. Teddy Bear collecting has not quite caught up with that hobby but we are gaining.

Just as there are miniaturists in the doll world, there are miniature Teddy Bear artists and makers as well. There is not a hard line drawn between miniature and standard sizes but generally speaking, anything in the range of 4 to 5in (10 to 13cm) tall starts to enter the magic world of the miniaturist. Even with our number of years in creating Teddy Bears, we are still in awe of the talented people who can craft these tiny miracles.

Several years ago we had the pleasure of meeting Sara Phillips of Maryland who is widely recognized as an outstanding miniature Teddy Bear artist. We asked her why she preferred to work with miniatures and she responded, "I love bears, period, but I've always been fascinated by tiny things. I thought it would be fun to try doing a miniature replica of a classic, jointed Teddy Bear. At the time that I started, I didn't know of anyone else doing this (although there were a few people out there) so it was kind of a challenge, too."

Elaine Fujita-Gamble of Seattle is another miniaturist with an enormous reputation. Elaine says, "I like making all sizes of bears, but my favorites are under 7in (18cm) because my least favorite part of bear making is stuffing the bears and small bears take very little time to stuff. Small bears also make fun traveling companions."

Another miniature bear artist whose fame is rapidly spreading is Dickie Harrison of Baltimore. "I make miniature bears," she says, "because I am

The multi-talented Beverly Port and Miss Emily, one of many outstanding creations by this internationally recognized authority. Photograph courtesy of Beverly Port.

basically a miniature enthusiast. I love miniature anything. I've always said if it's worth making at all, it's worth making in miniature. When Donna (daughter) brought her first bear home, the first thing I said was I wonder how small I can make one and keep the quality and proportion. For me, the 2½ to 3in (8cm) size is my specialty. I have always been fascinated with little duplicates and besides, they take up less space. Proportion of everything is the most important. That's the rule for a good little bear."

Two of Dickie's most important tools in her work are bent-nose tweezers for stuffing and a very small hemostat (surgical clamp). She says, "think small... small needles, small scissors. Use small stitches. Every stitch has to be perfect and that's why I do everything by hand."

Elaine Fujita-Gamble suggests using cotton batting from upholstery shops for stuffing miniatures as it is less expensive than fiberfill and packs firmer with less work. In a full-size Teddy it would not be as desirable as fiberfill, but many of the supplies and techniques in miniature making differ greatly from the full-size bear. For joints, Elaine suggests a small two-hole button joined with a cotter pin. Sara Phillips feels that one of her greatest assets is a good magnifying lamp. In addition to making her work easier, she finds it helps save her eyes from strain. Sara is constantly changing her techniques and feels that experimentation is very important.

Additional suggestions and guidelines for miniaturists can be found in other sections of this book.

Debonair Bear by Sara Phillips.

A mohair miniature by Elaine Fujita-Gamble.

Dickie Harrison's miniature Yes/No Teddy Bear.

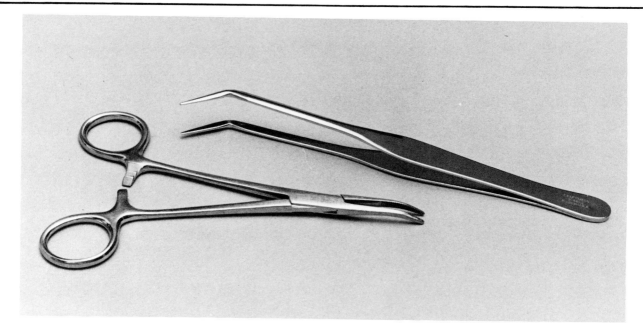

Hemostat (surgical clamp) and tweezers are a must for the miniature bear maker.

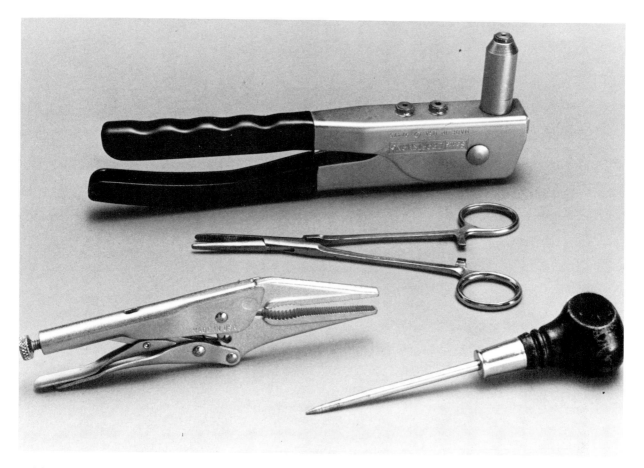

A hemostat (surgical clamp), scratch awl, long nose locking pliers and a rivet gun are indispensible tools.

A lighted magnifier saves eye strain.

Sir Edward II discovers a little friend. Miniature by Elaine Fujita-Gamble.

Chapter Three:
By The Yard Or By The Roll

As discussed in the previous chapter, Teddy Bears have been constructed in virtually every material imaginable. Our primary interest is in fabric Teddy Bears, and two categories exist under the heading of fabrics. We have man-made and natural fabrics, and within these categories are a host of fabrics that are most suitable for the making of Teddy Bears.

Man-made fabrics are the first choice of the mass producers because of their low cost and availability. Pile fabrics simulate the fur of the real bear and are produced in a rainbow of colors. The pile is made from synthetic fibers knitted into a yarn back. Major fibers used are polyester, acrylic and modacrylic. Backing yarns are polyester and olefin. Polyester fiber is primarily used in the manufacture of curled "shearling" look fabrics. Acrylics are used as a 100% pile or in combination with modacrylics for the "plush" look. They are usually added to provide the long fibers for the "Faux Fur" look.

Pile fabrics are made on specially designed knitting machines. The pile fibers are simultaneously knitted into the backing yarn. The weight of each fabric is determined by the amount of fiber that is fed into the machine. Generally speaking, the more dense or heavier the fabric, the higher the price per yard will be. Another key factor in determining the quality and, therefore, the price is finishing. It is a process of shearing and polishing the fibers. This process, along with carefully chosen blends of fiber, results in the desired "hand" or touch and appearance of the fabric.

Before processing the fibers, they are dyed in a wide range of colors from light pastels to deep earth tones, so the color selection available to the consumer is almost endless. Because of the sophistication of the new knitting machines, manufacturers can now produce various patterns as well.

There are only a handful of mills in the United States today that produce plush fabric. One of their major customers is the toy plush industry, but the pile is also used in a host of other products from clothing to automotive uses.

For the Teddy Bear maker, there are a number of sources for pile fabric. Most of the fabric store chains carry a good selection of plush in a wide variety of colors and densities. An advantage in buying from this type of store is that you can be reasonably sure of being able to get the same type and color over an extended time period.

Another source of plush for the bear maker are the fabric stores that specialize in close-outs. They buy roll ends and discontinued pieces from a variety of sources and are able to sell at lower prices. However, you have no assurance that you will be able to get that same material the next time you visit their store. This can be a problem if you are selling your Teddies to a number of retail stores where it is important to be able to supply the same plush on a continuing basis.

The artist-entrepreneur decides that the solution is to go directly to the manufacturer and buy direct. A shock sets in when our budding business person discovers that the mill is geared to selling in minimum quantities of 500 to 1000 yards per color! Good news is on the horizon, however, as some of the mills have recognized the small quantity demand and have set up departments or programs to sell at least some of their fabrics in much smaller quantities. Some of the plush manufacturers also have factory outlet stores at or near their mills, and the bear maker will generally find a good selection of fabrics that can be purchased in small quantities at substantial savings. Many of the new crop of suppliers to Teddy Bear makers are also offering domestic and imported man-made plush fabrics to their customers, along with imported mohair. Their prices are almost always based on the quantity you order. Buy a small amount and make a few bears before ordering in larger quantities.

Because almost all of the early Teddy Bears were made of mohair, the collector of contemporary Teddies most often wants the top quality that only mohair or a mohair blend can provide. Steiff, Hermann and many of the early Teddy Bear manufacturers have added mohair bears to their lines to meet this demand. The word "mohair" is actually a corruption of the Turkish word "mukhyar," meaning "the best of selected fleece." It is the fleece of the Angora goat, which grows in beautiful white lustrous locks. The most desirable fleece grows in ringlets. The fiber grows quite rapidly and the goats are shorn annually in Turkey, and twice a year in South Africa and the United States.

Even though this fleece grows at the rate of about 1in (3cm) per month on the goats raised here in this country, growing the mohair is no easy task. The Angora goat is a graceful, delicate animal. If they are exposed to excessive rain, they can contract pneumonia, and too little rain may cause them to die of thirst. Predators are also a problem to Angora goat farmers. They not only protect their flocks, but work diligently to preserve the purity of the breed and improve the fleece quality.

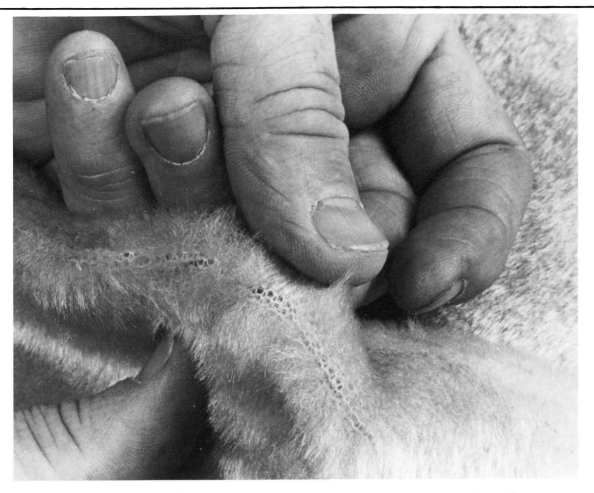

Check the plush fabric for density. The more dense fabrics may cost a little more, but they will produce a better quality Teddy Bear.

If you can brush back the pile and still not see the backing fabric, it will make into a beautiful bear.

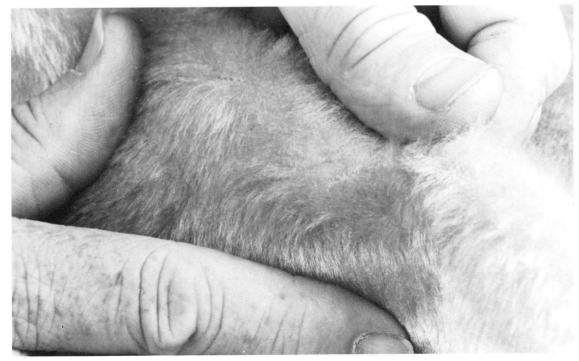

There are over 6 million Angora goats in the world, with a population of nearly 1½ million in Texas alone, where 96% of the total U.S. mohair is produced. This is due largely to the mild, dry climate and hilly, bushy terrain of Southwestern Texas, which is well suited to the health of the goat. In fact, the United States is the second largest producing nation in the world. Most of this output is shipped to processors outside the United States, where it is skillfully sorted, washed, combed spun and woven by craftsmen. The fiber's natural silky smooth characteristics allow it to dye easily. Mohair has mechanical properties very similar to wool, but slightly stronger. The medium and fine grades of mohair are used for making pile fabric with a cotton backing. Other uses for mohair include upholstery, hosiery, lightweight suitings and stoles. In spite of its delicate appearance, mohair is strong and durable. No wonder, then, the early mohair Teddy Bears were able to cope with the wear, tear and love they received.

The reason that 90% of the U.S. grown mohair is exported is that most American mills are geared towards using shorter fibers of 2in (5cm) or less, whereas mohair is used in 4 to 6in (10 to 15cm) lengths for processing. The low volume of mohair produced annually compared to cotton and wool requires smaller production runs and different technical expertise.

Finished mohair fabric suited for use by Teddy Bear makers is being imported from Europe and England. The artist is again faced with the same problem in buying direct from the mills, in that minimum orders are usually in the range of 100 to 200 yards per color, and at today's cost for mohair, this represents a substantial investment. You will find a number of suppliers to bear makers who offer a selection of mohair and mohair blends with prices based on the amount you order. It is still a wise decision to buy a small quantity to make sure it is of the quality you expect and looks great with your design before buying a substantial amount. It is particularly important to obtain samples to compare quality, as some producers sell mohair fabric that contains mohair, but it is woven into the backing very sparsely so that much of the backing shows. If you are going to pay for top quality, make certain it is top quality you are getting.

Several enterprising artists have found sources of used mohair, or mohair that came from an upholstered chair or davenport. It has the advantage of giving a Teddy Bear a slightly worn look and when you are fortunate enough to find it, the price is usually little or nothing, making the effort required to salvage it worthwhile. You will not be able to offer Teddies made in this fabric on a continuing basis, however.

Mohair blends are just as popular as the 100% mohair fabrics used in making Teddy Bears. The blend is not usually priced much lower, but it is much easier to work with than 100% mohair. Our experience with the fabric of complete mohair is

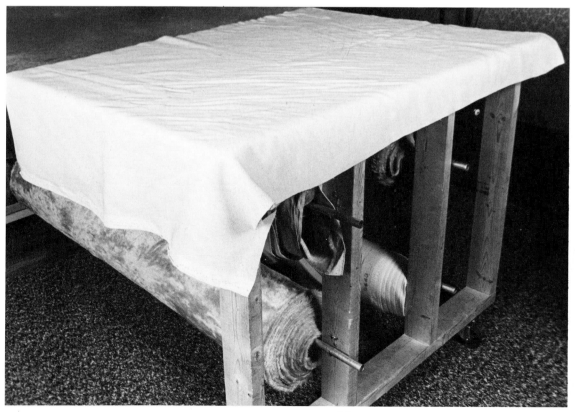

A cutting table with work area on top and storage for plush below.

44

A herd of Angora goats that look almost as cuddly as the mohair Teddy Bears produced from their fleece. Photograph courtesy of the Mohair Council of America.

shared by many Teddy Bear artists we have talked with. It is extremely difficult to hold in place when sewing; it slips badly. One artist who uses a commercial sewing machine told us that she has not experienced this problem on her machine. After our troublesome experience, we tried a mohair blend of 40% mohair, 30% wool and 30% rayon, and the results were much more satisfactory. The pile is extremely dense and reminds us a great deal of some of the magnificent Teddy Bears from the 1910 era in our collection.

The high cost of mohair in this country is due not only to the complex process of producing it, but the duty and shipping costs add as much as 25% by the time it is received. After you have purchased a small quantity and have decided that it will greatly enhance your Teddy Bears, you might want to consider placing a joint order with other artists and bear makers to allow you to buy in slightly larger quantities for a better price. Even though a number of people will make bears from the same fabric, they will all be highly individual, since the work of each artist is vastly different from another's.

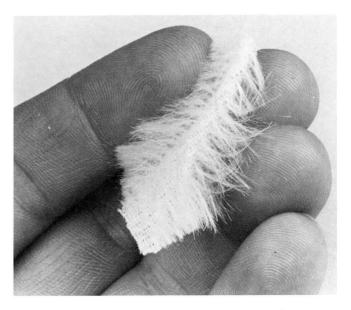

This material is classified as mohair, but the density is non-existant!

45

Chapter Four:
Supplies And Where To Find Them

Since this book is directed primarily to the Teddy Bear maker who works with plush materials, we will concentrate on the supplies used for this category. In the previous chapter we talked about where and how to buy plush, and some of those same principles apply to all other supplies as well. Everyone likes to save money, but it is false economy to buy a gross of eyes for bears if you only have potential of making a dozen Teddy Bears. Even if you perceive the need for larger quantities, start with just a few of an item to make sure it is going to do the job you intend it to do.

Hobby and hardware stores are an excellent source for some of the hand tools you will frequently use. Before investing in tools, however, you would do well to determine how frequently you plan to use the tool. If you only plan to make a few Teddies, then, by all means, buy an inexpensive tool or borrow one from a friend. If you are more serious about your endeavor and feel you will get good use from your investment, then buy a better quality that will hold up well to frequent use. The pages of *Teddy Bear and friends®* magazine feature ads from suppliers of bear making products. Probably one of the best sources for information and one of the most overlooked are other bear makers. It is true that some crafts persons are guarded when it comes to revealing their sources, but many more are very open and sharing with their information. If Teddy Bear making is going to be more than a passing fancy to you, you may want to investigate membership in the American Teddy Bear Artists Guild. They hold conferences in various sections of the country where seminars and workshops are keyed to members' needs. Details are available by writing to them at the address listed in the Important Addresses section at the back of the book.

When we started producing Teddy Bears for the commercial marketplace, we did not have the magazine and organizational resources that are available today. One of the greatest sources for information that we frequently used and continue to use is the Thomas Registry of United States Manufacturers, found in most public libraries. There you will discover a listing covering a dozen or so volumes of every conceivable product produced in this country. It was here that I found a company that would die cut joints for me. I had mixed emotions about this discovery, for although it meant I no longer had to spend endless hours in the basement cutting joints by hand, the minimum order required was 20,000 joints! To put that in better perspective,

they easily filled three large drums with the excess placed in two reasonably large cardboard boxes.

The Thomas Registry is listed by company and by product, and you have to use some ingenuity in making your search. There was no category for Teddy Bear joints, but searching through a section on die cutting products and stamping products provided a host of leads to follow. When writing for information, it would be wise to use a letterhead so that you present a professional image to the company you are writing to. Do not be discouraged if some of your letters go unanswered. Many of these companies simply are not in a position to deal with potential customers who will only be spending a few hundred dollars. We follow the theory that if you send enough letters to enough sources, you will sooner or later turn up what you need. Telephone calls can sometimes bring faster results, but be honest with the company you are calling and let them know right from the beginning that your resources are limited. Many of these people are willing to work with even the smallest customer and will extend you every courtesy given even their largest customer.

Teddy Bear collector clubs are also a great source of information. If there is not a club in your area, inquire about a doll collector's club. Many doll collectors are turning to Teddy Bear collecting;

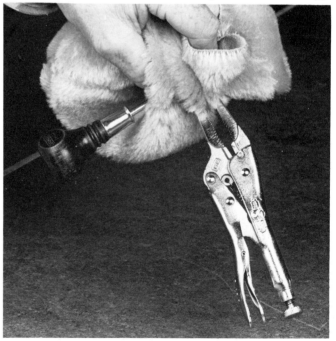

A scratch awl and locking pliers make a perfect combination for installing joints.

some of the same supplies and tools used by doll hobbyists can be used by the bear maker as well.

Do not hesitate to discuss your needs with people who are totally unrelated to the Teddy Bear collecting world. Early in our work I had a need for a special tool that simply was not available. In a discussion with an acquaintance, I explained my problem and my friend not only suggested the solution, but had the necessary equipment to produce exactly the tool I needed. He was not a Teddy Bear collector but he had two children, so we agreed on a trade of two Teddy Bears for a one-of-a-kind tool. In fact, you will be surprised how often you can arrange a barter. Would you believe we traded a Teddy Bear for a ride in a hot air balloon? Admittedly, there was more than a stroke of luck in that coincidence but it does not hurt to ask.

A great tip on buying supplies comes from Teddy Bear artist Sharon July, creator of those adorable Pine Forest Bears. Sharon says, "ordering supplies by mail and having them shipped directly to you is a savings of time. Shipping charges are more than offset by what you save in gas. Think about how many bears you could make during the time used driving after supplies and standing in line. Your time is very valuable. Sometimes saving pennies costs you dollars in profits."

Elaine Fujita-Gamble finds surplus outlets are a great source for supplies in her miniature bear making. She gets washers, cotter pins and fiberboard to cut joints from one such outlet. Dickie Harrison, another miniaturist, gets her 1/2in (1cm) cotter pins from an auto supply dealer. She even has a button manufacturer that makes a one-hole button for her to use for joints!

One of the best sources for establishing contact with a number of people selling supplies is at Teddy Bear shows and doll shows. In addition to the dealers who deal in supplies exclusively, many of the Teddy Bear specialty shops and artist/bear makers selling bears also sell supplies. Investigate what they are offering and try them out. If it suits your needs, you can follow Sharon July's time-saving tip and continue to buy by mail.

Now let us cover some specific sources for specific items. If you have need for one or two pair of glass eyes, visit your local taxidermist, where you will find a variety of sizes and colors in bird and small animal eyes. Be sure to take your bear along to get the proper size. If you need larger quantities, check out a Teddy Bear supply source for your best price. Plastic eyes can be obtained from most hobby stores. Again, it you need quantity, check with a bear maker supply source.

Teddy Bear joints are made in plastic and hardboard. The plastic style, found in some hobby shops, have a stem attached to one disc that simply pushes into a hole in the second disc, locking in place. They are made in a variety of sizes and are simple to use. On the negative side, we have talked with bear makers who claim the plastic joints do not tighten up enough to make a snug joint. The previous suggestion holds that it is wise to try a few before investing in a large number.

Most Teddy Bear makers are using the hardboard style of joint because they are readily available or because they can cut their own. We used a circle cutter from the local hardware store to cut hardboard (tempered Masonite) joints for the first year. We still use this tool to cut special sizes. The hardboard joint is sometimes joined or fastened in place with a locking nut and bolt arrangement but if you are making a number of bears, this can be an expensive approach. Almost all antique Teddy Bears were joined with a cardboard and cotter pin combination. The only positive thing I can say about a cotter pin fastener is that it is inexpensive. They can be difficult to install and what is worse, the joints are almost impossible to make uniformly tight. Too little pressure and the limb falls limp. Too much pressure and the cotter pin pulls right through the joint.

We very early on decided that although we generally follow the old way of doing things when it comes to bear making, this is one area that needed modern technology. Thomas Registry to the rescue! Several hours of research and several weeks of letter writing produced a company that had the perfect solution. The listing for this company was under the heading "Fasteners," with a sub category of "Rivets." The solution is a device widely used in industry called a "Pop Rivet." Visit your local hardware store and ask to see the pop rivets and tools. While they are readily available in a variety of sizes, we prefer to buy an aluminum rivet in a longer size than you can find in most hardwares. The aluminum rivet can be installed without requiring a great deal of strength, and the extra long size allows

Thomas Register at the library is an ideal source for many supplies.

us to use one size for all the bears we make, from 13in (33cm) all the way up to our 37in (94cm) Teddy. Our Chapter titled "Bear Under Construction" gives the detailed step-by-step procedure in using our riveted system. In order to obtain the extra long size rivet, we were again faced with the need to buy in significantly large quantities. Since this has become a factor with more and more of the supplies we use, we have recently branched into selling bear making supplies to other bear makers. This not only allows us to obtain the larger quantities at a more economical price, but it adds another dimension to our business operation. This same approach can be accomplished by joining with other bear makers to buy some of your needs together. The other bear makers in your area can become strong allies in many ways.

Die-cut hardboard discs come in a variety of sizes for putting joints in Teddy Bears.

Thomas Register listings are arranged with sub categories.

Printed letterheads will give your operation a professional touch.

49

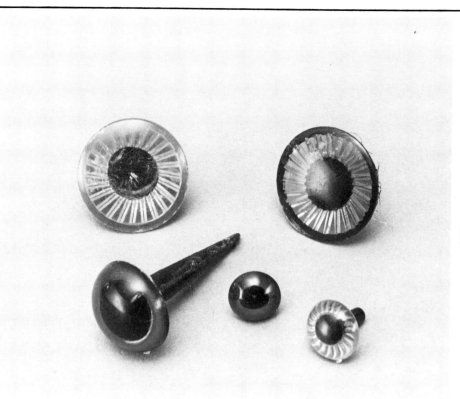

Plastic eyes are made in many sizes, colors and styles.

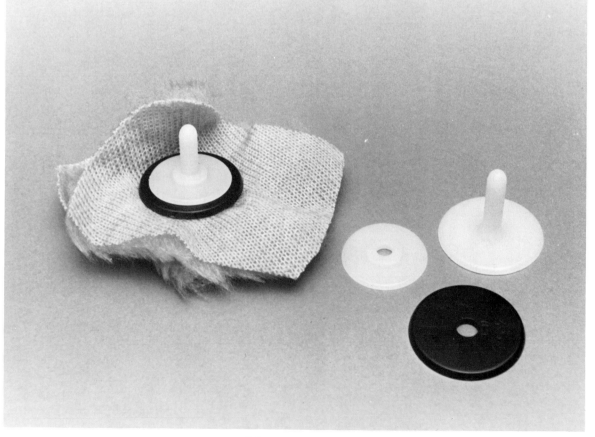

Plastic joints are made in several styles.

A hole cutter adjusts to any size up to 2½in (6cm) for cutting your own joints.

The hole cutter requires a drill press for maximum efficiency.

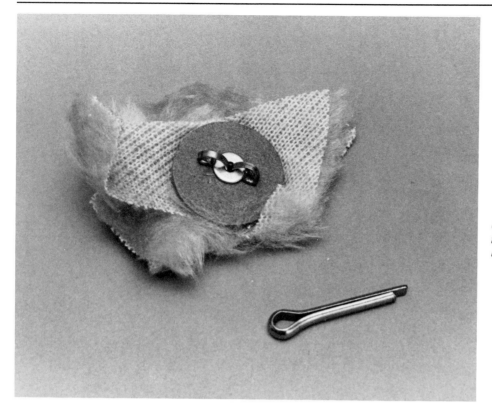

Cotter pin joints are difficult to install and generally result in a loose joint.

Rivet guns are easy to use and available at most hardware and department stores.

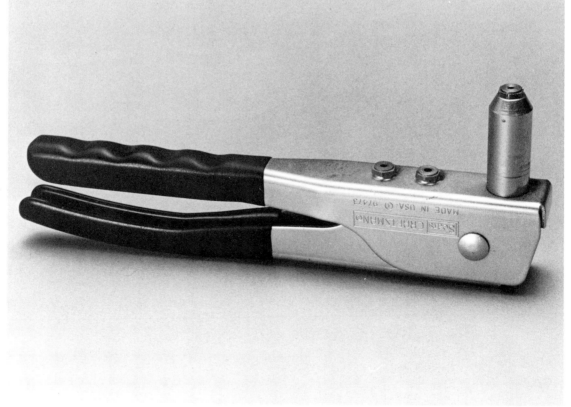

Chapter Five:
My Bear By Design

Designing and making your own Teddy Bear will provide you with some of the most frustrating, time-consuming and discouraging experiences you will encounter in handcrafting Teddy Bears. Yet it is without question one of the most rewarding projects you can imagine. How does one design their own Teddy Bear? Part of the process is a learned experience, and part is a talent that lies within. The more successful artist has an ability to create a mind's eye view of the finished work and to follow logical steps to that end. It is also a tremendous amount of trial and error. This experimentation is minimal with some, but for most of us it can be very time consuming.

Before you get caught up in developing your own patterns, it is imperative that you handcraft several Teddy Bears by following commercial patterns. In fact, the more experience you have in this area, the better your chances are for successfully creating your own Teddy Bear.

Begin your design work by studying a variety of patterns featured in books, including the pattern we have provided you with in this book. Cut out all of the pieces and lay them out on a table and compare one pattern with another. It will make your study easier if you select patterns for bears of the same type (jointed) and of approximately the same size.

Since the character and charm of most Teddy Bears is closely tied to the design of the head, you can minimize some of the experimental time by starting with the head design. Once you have made a head that has the desired appeal, you can then proceed with the rest of the Teddy.

Using our head pattern as the basis, draw the outline on paper. Want a longer nose? Try extending the pattern as in **Figure 1**. Bear in mind (no pun intended) that you will need to extend the gusset proportionately (**Figure 2**).

Perhaps you want the nose fatter as well as longer. Try the approach shown in **Figure 3**.

Feel your Teddy should have more of a forehead? **Figure 4** will take you in that direction.

We should give a word of caution at this point that you should not make too many changes in the pattern design without trying them in fabric. Otherwise you will lose the feel of molding your mind's eye image into the final form. You will be amazed at how much difference a subtle change in the pattern will make in the finished bear. Also remember to make note of any changes you make when you are actually sewing on the fabric. You may have discovered, for example, that your gusset is a bit too long, so you simply trim it with scissors at the sewing machine. Trim the pattern as well.

A drafting table is ideal for design work but a table top will do just as well.

The bear's head does not have to be completely assembled and finished to give you a feel for his appearance. Sewing the parts, stuffing, inserting eyes and pinning on ears will give you the basic idea of what you have created. If he is starting to look good, proceed with nose and mouth to finish him. If not, back to the drawing board!

The body can give you added opportunity to give your bear character. If your Teddy is going to end up in costume as a grandpa, you may want to give him a pot belly. We have modified our body pattern in **Figure 5** to show you one way of accomplishing this.

If you decide your Teddy's body needs to be longer, it may require that you lengthen the arms as well. You can certainly change his appearance by making the body longer and the legs shorter. The point we want to stress is do not be afraid to experiment. As we stated in the beginning of this chapter, you will very likely spend endless, frustrating hours trying to go from what your mind views to a pattern and finally to cloth.

In experimenting with design, look at the possibility of reducing the number of pieces needed for the completed bear. Perhaps you can lay out a body that has two pieces instead of four. It may save time in cutting and in sewing, which means your labor costs are reduced. Since the labor cost is much higher than the cost of the materials, it is a good area to examine for savings.

You should also consider what effect adding pieces to your design might have. It may not reduce your costs, but consider the possibility that it may strongly enhance the quality of your finished Teddy and, therefore, make him more marketable.

After many hours or many months, whatever the case may be, you have completed a Mona Lisa in plush and now must consider whether you should obtain a copyright on your work. First, consider what you plan to do with your design. If you are going to make some bears in your spare time, selling them at craft markets or in a limited number by mail, then the time and expense may not be worthwhile. If you want the copyright to enable you to sell your design to a major producer, you should be aware that few if any manufacturers will be interested in it. Most plush producers of any size employ full-time designers to create products based on their manufacturing abilities.

Your best opportunity for turning your creative skills into extra cash will probably be in making the product and selling it. It may still be desirable to register a copyright. Due to a change in the copyright law in 1978, you are not required to register for a copyright, as it is automatically secured when the work is created. There are advantages to registration, however. It establishes a public record of your claim and may be of great value in the event of a legal dispute. The copyright protection will cover your work for your lifetime plus an additional 50 years. The work of the Teddy Bear artist can be covered by copyright under the visual arts category. Registering your copyright can be taken care of by an attorney, or you may wish to file the application yourself. In either case it would be worthwhile to make a visit to your library to research the subject. Be certain the book you select contains updated information on the changes made in the copyright law in 1978. You can also obtain information directly from the Copyright Office. The address is listed in the Important Addresses section at the back of this book.

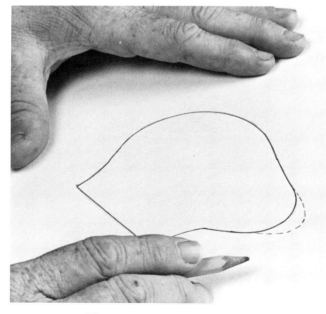

Figure 1. Extending the nose.

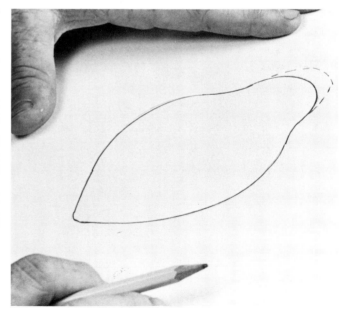

Figure 2. Do not forget to extend the Gusset proportionately.

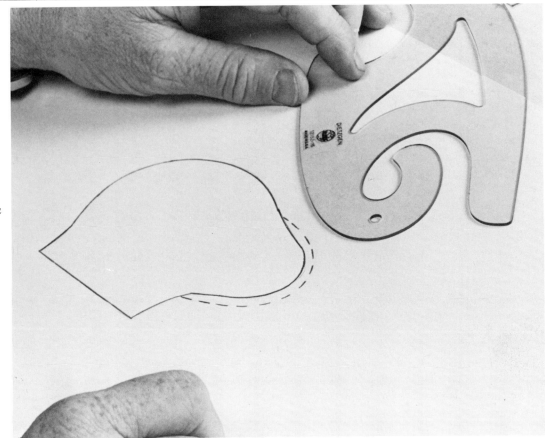

Figure 3. *Making a fatter nose.*

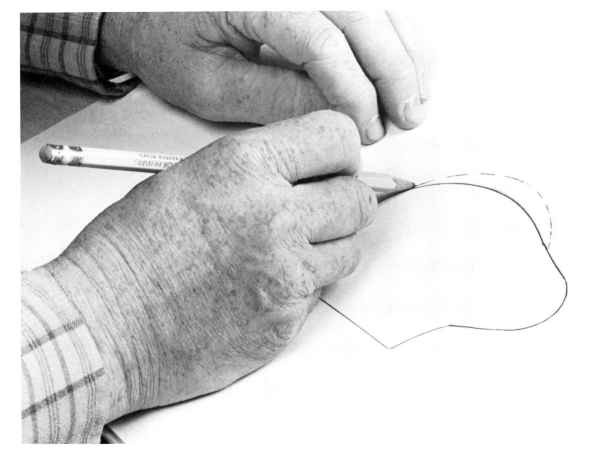

Figure 4. This results in a higher forehead.

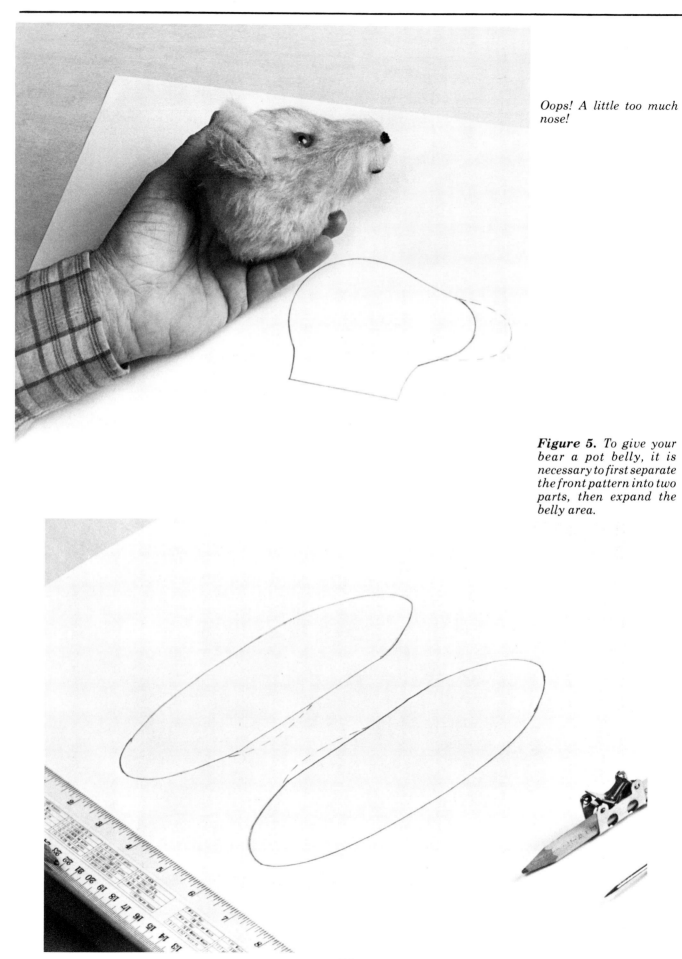

*Oops! A little too much
nose!*

Figure 5. *To give your
bear a pot belly, it is
necessary to first separate
the front pattern into two
parts, then expand the
belly area.*

Chapter Six:
Bear Under Construction

Teddy looks excited as he nears completion.

A simple "Bag" bear (a reference to a bear without joints) may require but a few pieces of fabric to construct, where the more complex jointed Teddies might require 20 or more pieces. We recognize that most collectors have a strong preference for the jointed Teddies, and yet we wanted this project to be as easy as possible to accommodate a larger number of bear makers. To accomplish this, we have simplified the more complex pattern to provide you with a fully-jointed Teddy Bear pattern that does not require any unusual or advanced skills. There are 14 pieces in all.

To construct a Teddy Bear, 12in (31cm), from our illustrated pattern, you will need the following tools:

A pair of needlecraft scissors (4¾in [12cm] long) normally used in embroidery and detail work

Dressmaker's straight pins

Interface (lightweight) to trace pattern

Fine point marking pen

Size 16 sewing machine needle for heavyweight woven fabric

100% polyester thread in color to match selected fabric

2 hardboard discs 2in (5cm) in diameter with 1/8in (.3cm) center hole

8 hardboard discs 1½in (4cm) in diameter with 1/8in (.3cm) center hole

5 cotter pins 1½in (4cm) long

10 flat washers with 1/8in (.3cm) center hole

Note: you may wish to substitute plastic joints

1 pair locking pliers

1 pair long nose pliers

1 scratch awl

Pastel chalk

1 bag polyester fiberfill

Wooden chopstick or small wooden spoon (for stuffing)

Selection of hand needles, including large eye needle to accommodate embroidery thread

T-pins

Embroidery floss (6 strand), color optional

1 pair glass or plastic eyes

Note: The mohair bear and the acrylic bear made from our pattern use 12 millimeter size, the white cashmere bear uses 10 millimeter shoe button style, and our patchwork quilt bear sports a pair of genuine antique shoe buttons.

Stiff bristle brush

1/4yd (23cm) plush fabric (minimum 48in [122cm] wide)

To dramatically illustrate the various appearances your Teddy Bear can take depending on the material you select, we have constructed four bears, all using the same pattern presented here. The first bear is made of a mohair blend of 40% mohair, 30% wool and 30% rayon. The top bears in our line are made from this material. Next, we have a Teddy made from a deep brown acrylic plush, typical of the material found in neighborhood fabric stores. Our third bear is made from an 80-year-old family heirloom quilt. Now we would be the last people in the world to cut up a beautiful treasure, but this unfortunate quilt was literally falling apart, with gaping holes everywhere. We did not have the heart to toss it out, and thank goodness we saved it, for there was ample material to produce another family heirloom. Our fourth Teddy for the project was made from a beautiful white cashmere wool fabric we picked up several years ago at a discount fabric shop. The price was just too good to pass up, so we purchased a few yards and tucked it away for future use.

As you study the bears (see page 64), it is difficult to believe they all came from the same pattern. We have used one ear pattern on two of them and the larger pattern on the other two. Slightly different eyes, eye placement and embroidery thread color and design (some horizontal noses and some vertical) were employed to further illustrate how small changes can make a difference in the outcome.

Before beginning this project, read the instructions all the way through from start to finish. You may find that you have some of the tools and supplies on hand and may wish to substitute them for those on the list. Our instructions and illustrations are based on the use of 1/4in (.7cm) nap mohair blend. However, if you have never worked with a mohair material, we strongly recommend you select an acrylic fabric for this project to avoid a costly mistake on expensive mohair. Once you have completed a Teddy Bear to your satisfaction, you can then repeat the project with mohair.

In selecting your fabric, check the backing to make sure it does not stretch excessively, as this will distort the bear's features and size during stuffing.

Lay the interface over the printed pattern and copy it with a marking pen. Be sure to mark the arrows on the interface.

Cut out each piece.

Lay the fabric on a flat surface (table or floor) with the pile side up. Test with your hand to make sure the nap runs toward you (from top to bottom). This direction may vary from one fabric to another. Once you have determined this, turn the fabric over and make an arrow with chalk in the direction of the pile. This will now correspond with the arrows on the pattern.

Lay the pattern pieces on the material with the arrows facing down (in the direction of the nap).

Pin the pattern pieces to the fabric and cut. It is important to cut the backing only and not the pile, so there is enough fur to cover the seams. This is the reason for using small, sharp scissors. You will have 14 pieces when you finish.

All machine sewing will be done on the backing side of the material. Pinning the pieces before sewing will help to avoid shifting of the material. Always leave a 1/4in (.7cm) seam.

Sew gusset side A to left head side A.

Sew gusset side B to right head side B, leaving open where marked.

Sew left head side C to right head side C. Clip the neck in the 3 places indicated.

Fold body front at center and sew seam D to seam D at top and bottom.

Join body backs together at top and bottom seam E, leaving open where marked.

Sew body front to body back all around seam F, matching top and bottom. The completed body will look like a deflated football.

Fold a leg at center and sew seam G along the side and across the bottom of the foot, leaving an opening at top where indicated. Clip the ankle in the 3 places indicated.

Sew the second leg in the same manner.

Fold an arm at center and sew seam H from one side to the other, leaving an opening at top where indicated.

Repeat with second arm.

Select the ear pattern you want (large or small) and sew two pieces along seam I, leaving open where marked.

Repeat with second ear.

You have now completed the machine sewing portion of the project. Turn all of the pieces right side out except the body.

The body must now be marked with joint locations for arms and legs. To mark the location of the arms, make sure the body is right side up by locating the hump. From the center of the top, measure 2½in (6cm) down a side seam and mark the location with chalk. Avoid using a marking pen as it may show through the material.

Mark the opposite side seam in the same manner.

Turn the body upside down to mark the leg locations. From the bottom center seam, measure 1½in (4cm) along the side seam and mark the location.

Mark the opposite side seam in the same manner.

Turn the body right side out.

Push the scratch awl through the hole in a 2in (5cm) disc.

Place the disc through the opening at the back of the body and use the scratch awl to locate a point on the front seam 1/4in (.7cm) ahead of the center. Push the scratch awl through the seam at that point until the disc is snug against the inside body.

Slide the other 2in (5cm) disc inside the head and center it at the base.

Push the scratch awl through the base of the head into the center hole of the second disc.

Holding them in alignment, clamp them together with the locking pliers. Now you can remove the scratch awl.

Place a washer on the cotter pin and insert it through the center hole where the scratch awl was located.

Slide a washer on the opposite side of cotter pin so that you now have a washer on each side of the joint.

Holding the cotter pin in place, use the long nose pliers to bend one side of the cotter pin away from the hole. You will note that the end of the cotter pin is cut so that one side is slightly longer than the other, allowing you to grip it with the pliers. If you have difficulty gripping just one side, use a knife to slide in between and force one side away from the other.

Bend one side of the cotter pin in a loop until it is snug.

Bend the other side of the cotter pin in the opposite direction until it, too, is snug. You can now release the locking pliers.

Slide a 1½in (4cm) disc inside the opening in the arm and locate it so you have 3/8in (1cm) of material above it for the shoulder seam.

With the back of the body facing up, lay the arm on the left side with the arm seam facing up.

Push the scratch awl through the center hole of the disc and through the arm fabric in the direction of the body.

Locate the arm mark on the inside of the body and push the scratch awl through the seam.

Place another disc inside the body and slide it onto the scratch awl until the two discs are aligned and snug. Clamp them in place with the locking pliers.

Follow the same procedure to install the cotter pin as you did for the head.

Install the second arm in the same manner, being sure the arm seam faces the back of the body.

Install each leg in the same manner, being certain that the feet face foreward. (Don't laugh; we have done it backwards!)

We now have a completely jointed Teddy and are ready to stuff him. This is best accomplished by using small quantities of fiberfill to avoid gaps.

Stuff the limbs first, using the chopstick or wooden spoon to push the fiberfill snugly in place. We prefer packing the stuffing tightly to give the firm feel of the antique bears, but you may stuff it to your own preference.

Stuff the arms, legs and body, leaving the head until last. Stuff the nose and bridge of the nose so that approximately one-third of the head is filled.

Placing the eyes is next, and their location can dramatically alter the appearance of the finished bear. We have located our eyes 1½ to 1⅝in (4cm) from the tip of the nose along the gusset seam. You may wish to experiment with this by holding the eyes in a desired location to see how he looks.

If you are using glass eyes on a wire stem, push the ends of the wire through the fabric and the fiberfill and twist them together inside the head. The fiberfill will help to hold the wires separate so the eyes stay in alignment. You will want to make at least five twists to make sure they are firmly anchored. This should draw the eyes into the head slightly to give a desirable appearance. If you have selected plastic eyes, follow the directions of the manufacturer for installation. You can now finish stuffing the head.

For those among you who plan to produce more than just a few Teddy Bears, you may want to consider our system of riveted joints. It is one area where modern technology has greatly improved on the old system of cotter pin fastening. The procedure is exactly the same as we described for using cotter pins, but you substitute the use of a 1/8in (.3cm) diameter pop rivet. They can be installed with a hand gun, or you can use more sophisticated electric or pneumatic guns for mass production work. The hand gun is an inexpensive tool available at most hardware stores. Although rivets are available in aluminum or steel, we prefer the aluminum rivet as most women find it easy to install, where the steel rivet requires a slightly stronger grip. While the rivets are normally sold in an adequate length (1/2in [1cm]), we purchase a special 3/4in (2cm) length that we use for all size bears. This compensates for longer plush that makes a wider gap between discs. Unfortunately, buying this special size requires us to purchase in quantities of 8000

rivets. To enable us to buy these and other supplies in quantity, we sell in reduced quantities to other artists and bear makers. You may want to consider this approach, or you may want to form a co-op with several bear makers in your area to take advantage of volume purchases at lower prices.

If you feel the riveted joint system we have developed may be of use in your work, visit your local hardware store and ask them to show you how it works. The hand guns are available in a standard model, suitable for most bear makers, or in a heavy duty model for the large volume producer. One word of caution. Be sure to purchase the washers made by the same company that makes the rivets. They are sometimes called back-up plates, and are machined for a close tolerance fit with the rivet. If you substitute a washer made by some other company, it may not work properly with the rivet. This advice comes from our experience in substituting washers because they were lower in price. The initial savings can be costly in the long run. We were fortunate to discover our error after just a few joints. We have used this method for over five years now, and in the course of producing thousands of Teddy Bears, we have only had three returned due to a joint failure. We think that is a record any manufacturer would be proud to achieve.

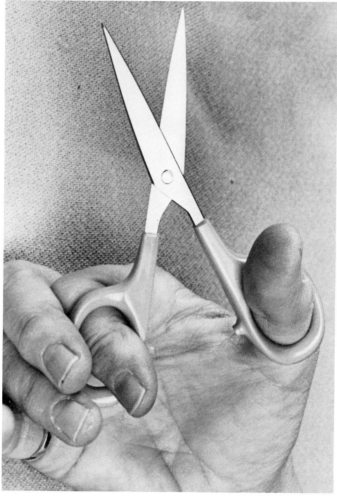

Small scissors give you more control in cutting the backing only.

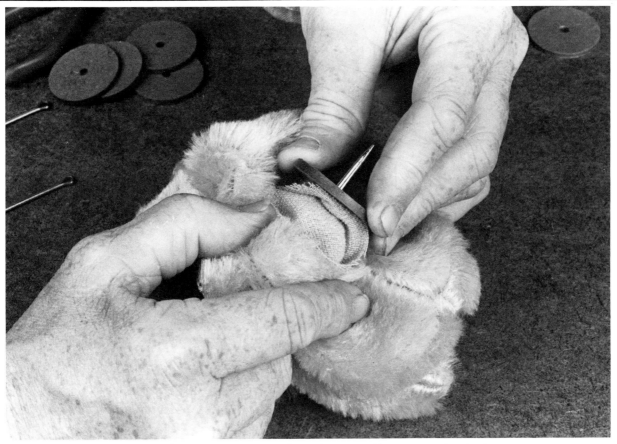

Movable joints are not as difficult to install as you might think.

Long nose locking pliers are preferable to the standard blunt nose type.

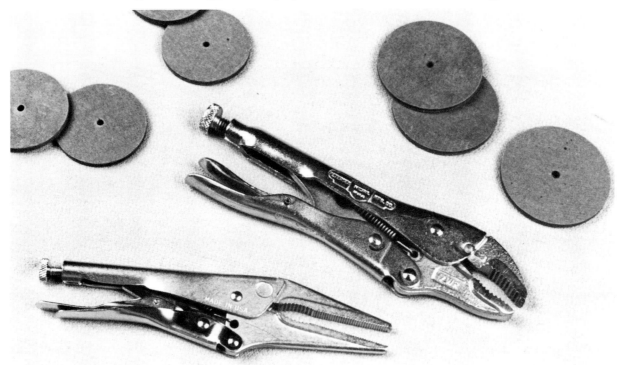

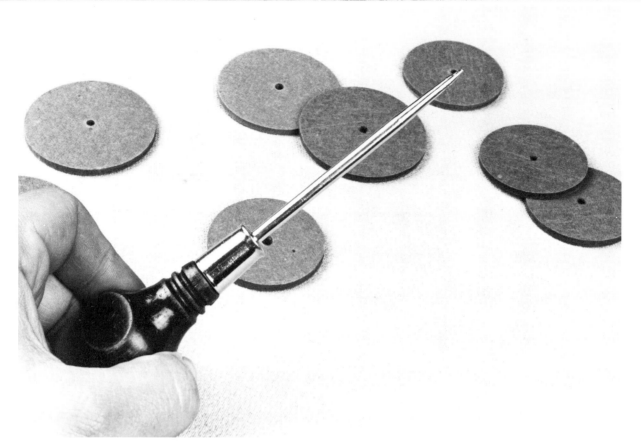

Make sure your scratch awl has a dull point to avoid poking a finger.

Keep a mental image of the completed bear in your mind so the arms end up at the top end, facing in, and the legs end up on the bottom, facing forward!

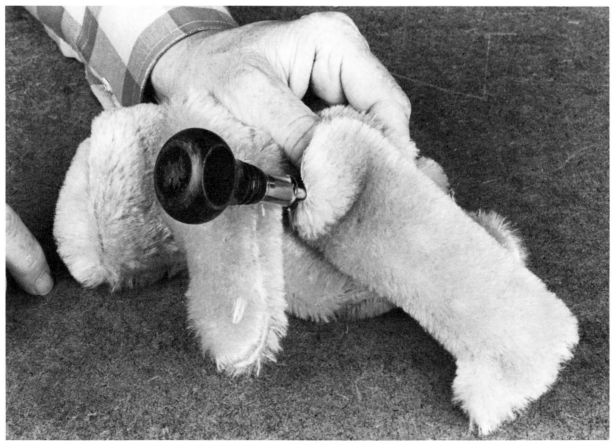

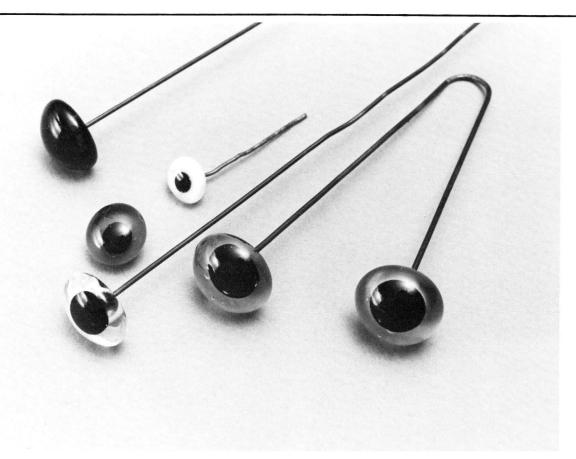

Glass eyes usually come on a wire stem.

A small brass bristle appliance brush is perfect for brushing out seams.

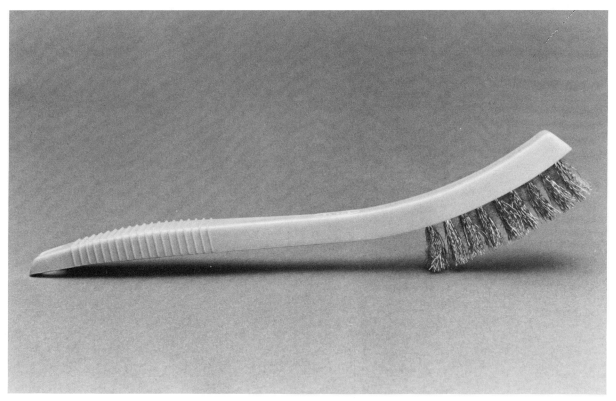

Four unique Teddies, all from one pattern.

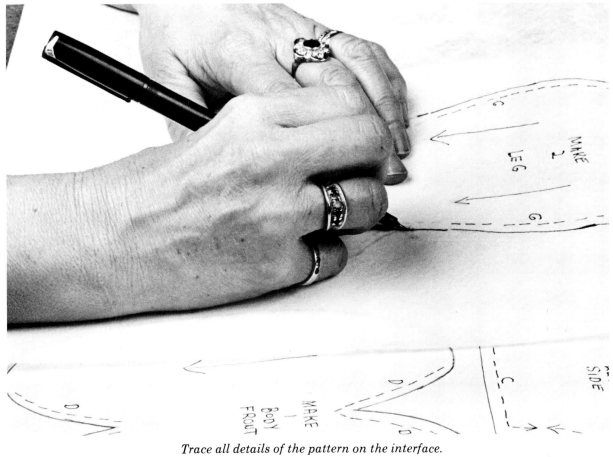

Trace all details of the pattern on the interface.

Carefully cut out each piece you have traced.

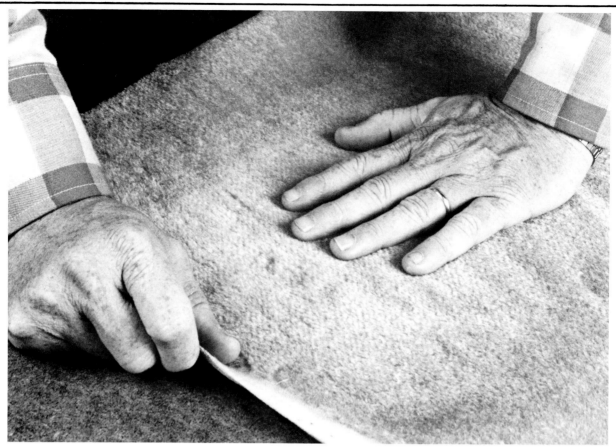

Determine the direction of the nap.

Mark the nap direction on the back side with chalk.

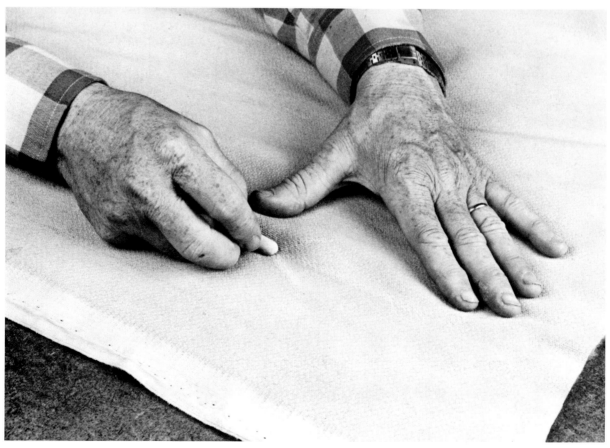

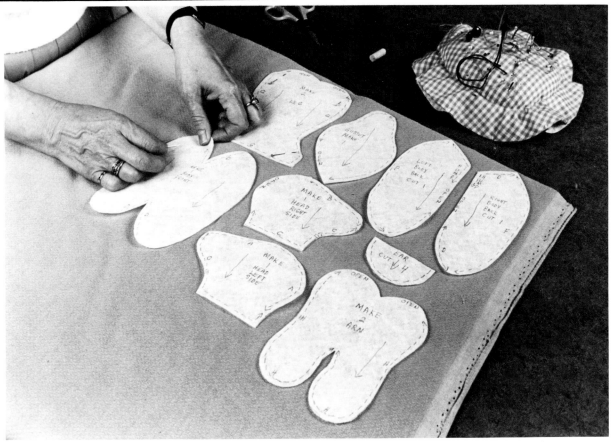

Lay out the pattern pieces efficiently to avoid scrap. Arrows go in the same direction as the nap.

Pin and cut each piece.

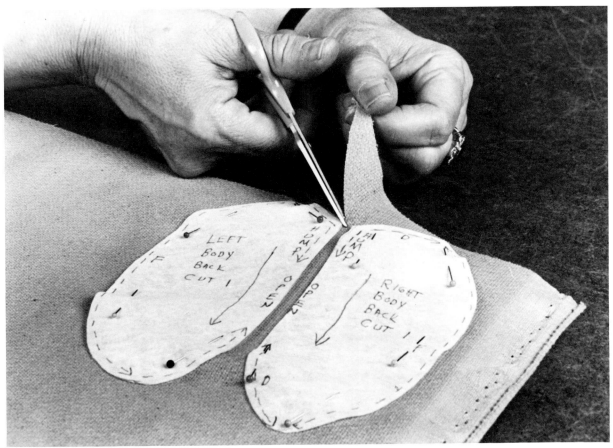

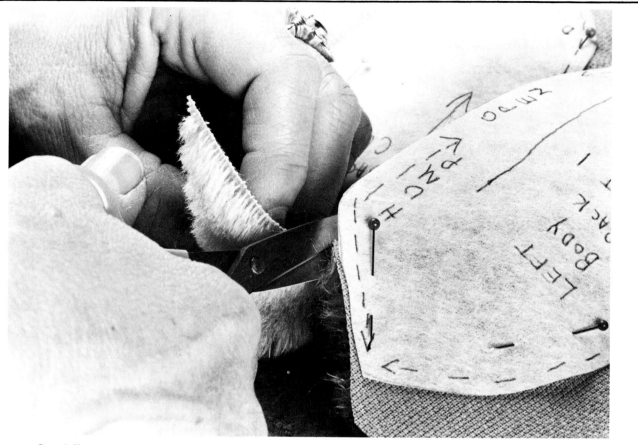

Carefully guide the lower cutting edge of the scissors through the nap so you cut only the backing.

Sew gusset side A to left head side A.

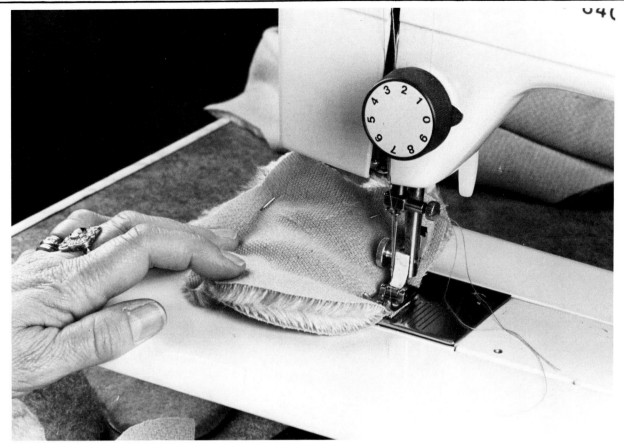

Sew gusset side B to right head side B. Leave open where marked.

Sew left head side C to right head side C.

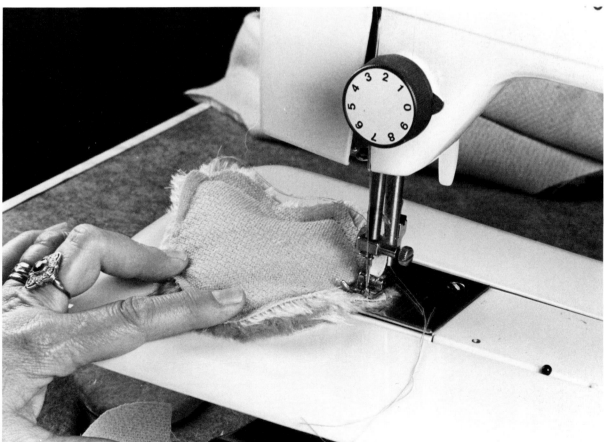

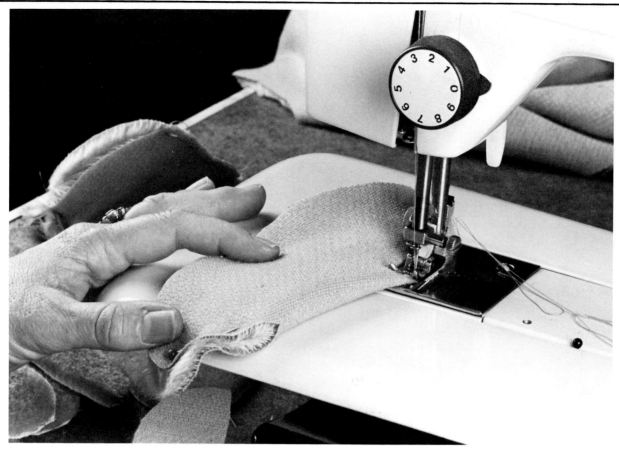

Fold body front at center and sew seam D to seam D at top and bottom.

Join body backs together at top and bottom seam E. Leave open where marked.

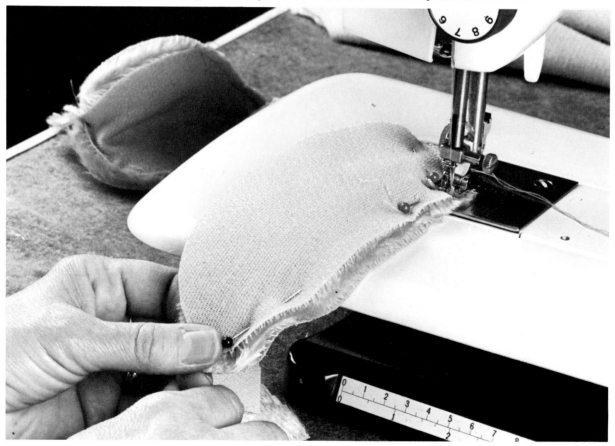

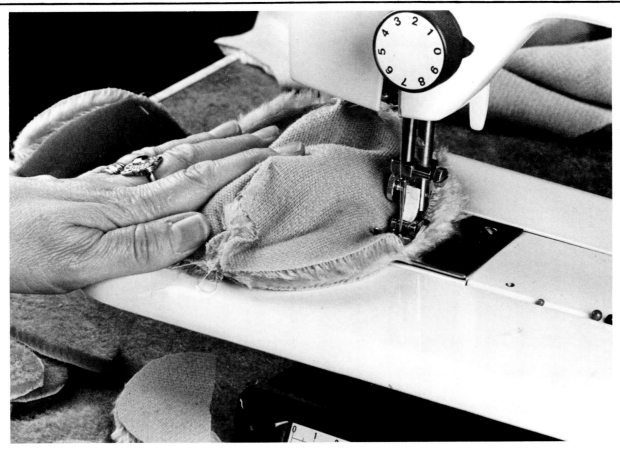

Sew body front to body back all around seam F, matching top and bottom.

Body is now complete.

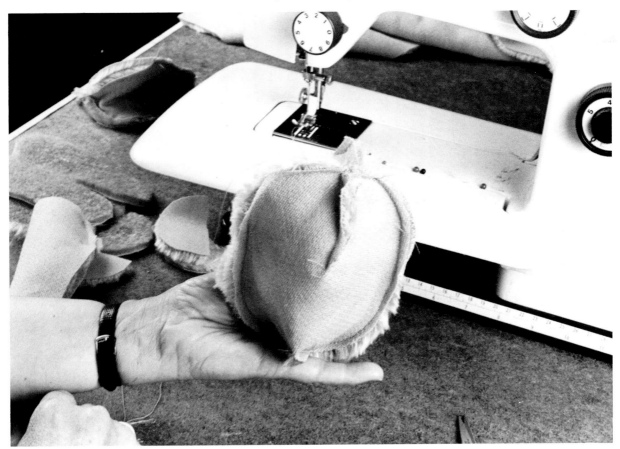

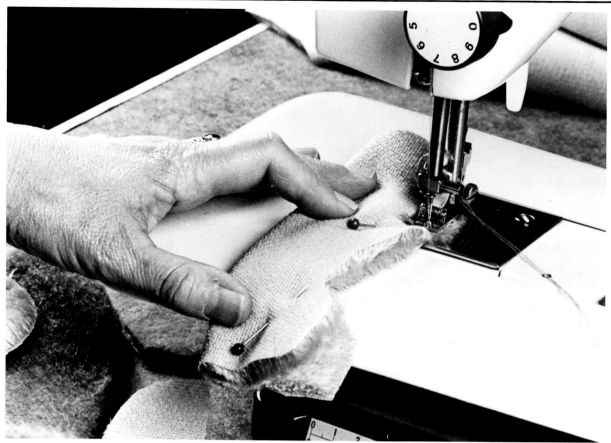

Fold leg at center and side and bottom.

Clip the ankle in the three places indicated.

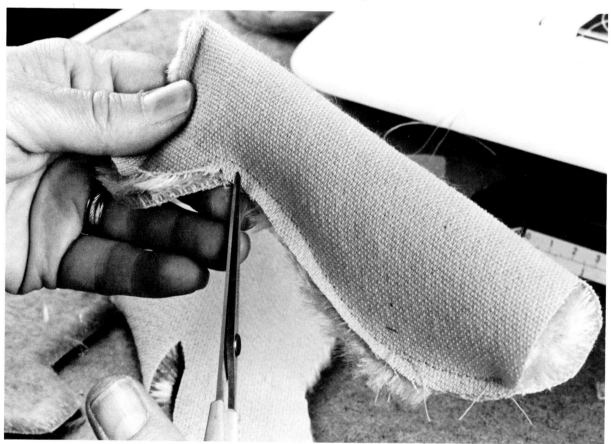

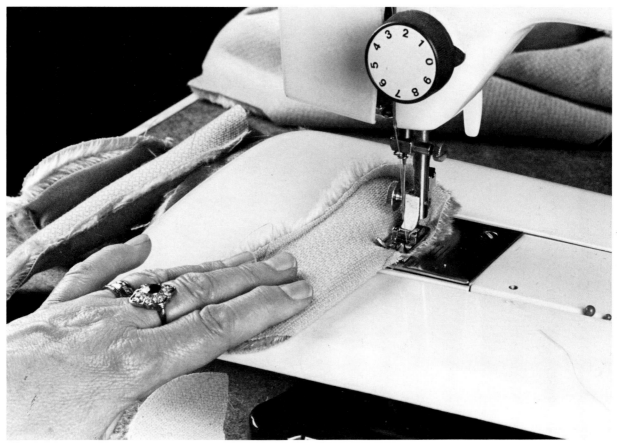

Fold arm at center and sew seam H from one side to the other. Leave open at top.

Turn the pieces right side out.

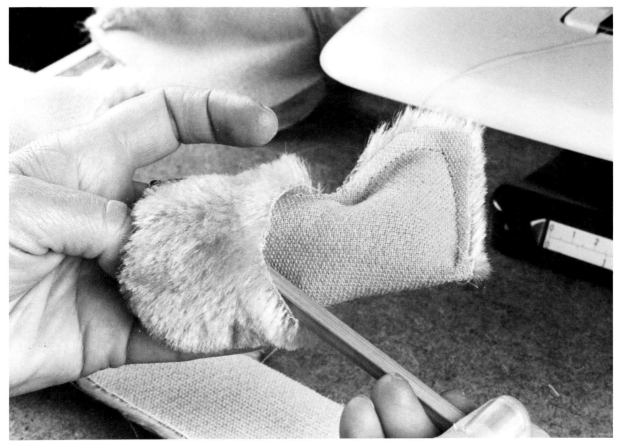

Now we are ready to put joints in.

Measure and mark the joint locations.

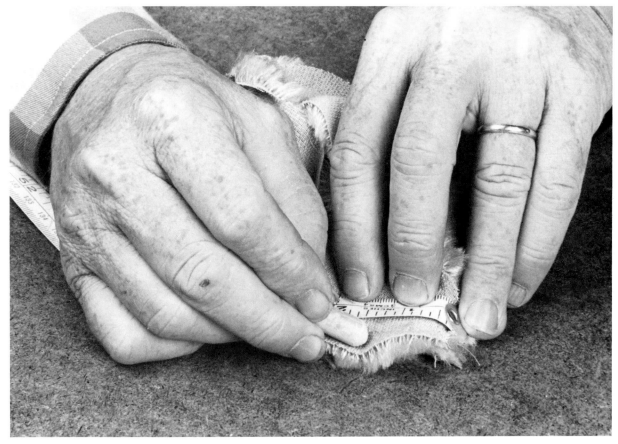

As you mark the joint locations, visually inspect the body to see that the arms and legs are going to be even.

Slide the large disc onto the scratch awl.

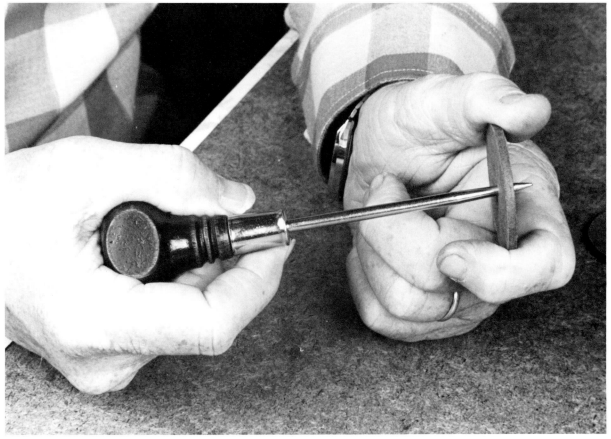

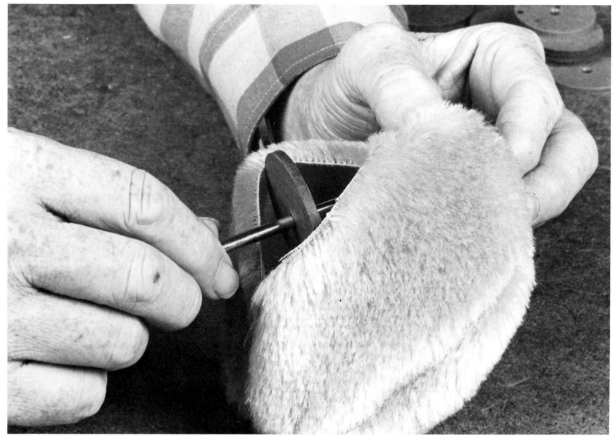

Enter through the body opening at the back to install the first head joint.

Push the scratch awl through the front seam just ahead of the point where all seams are joined.

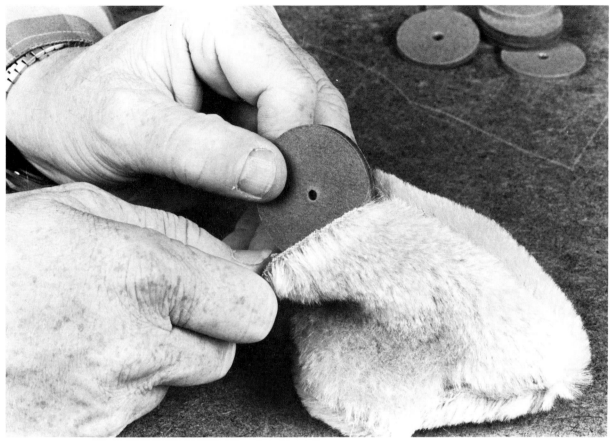

Place the matching disc inside the head at the bottom. Make sure the front bottom corner is covered by the disc to avoid an "Adam's apple" on your bear.

Align head and body discs with scratch awl.

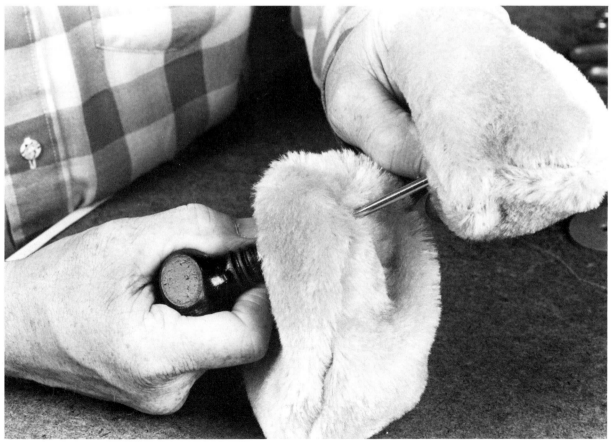

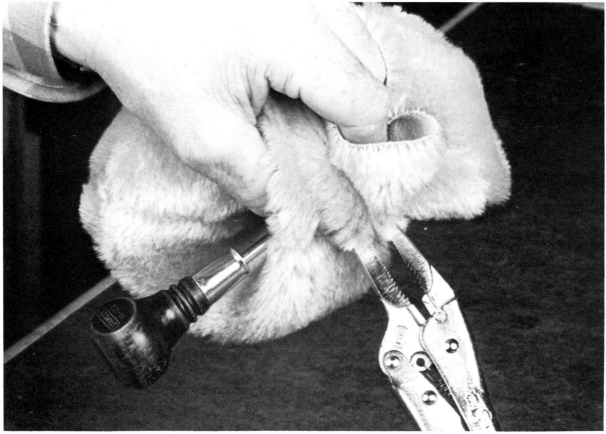

Clamp the aligned discs with locking pliers. Remove scratch awl.

Cotter pin with washer in place.

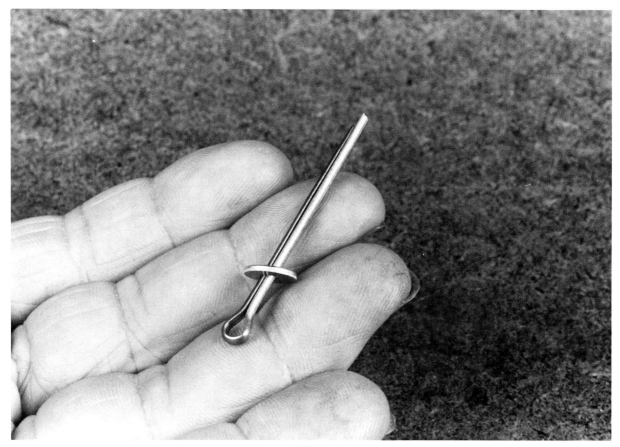

78

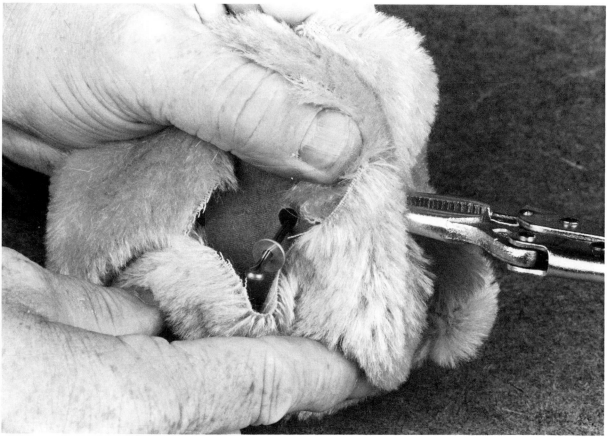

Insert cotter pin through center hole in aligned discs.

Slide a second washer in place on opposite side of joint.

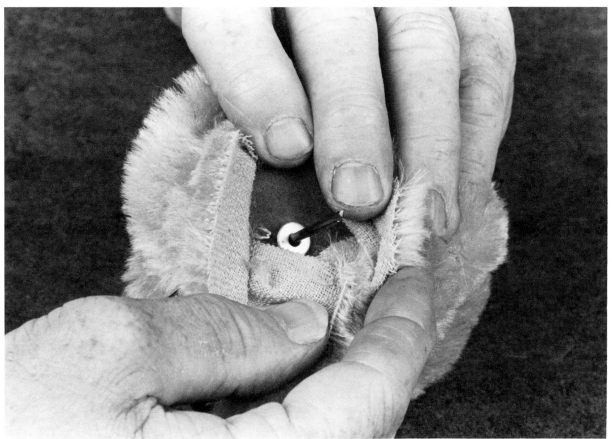

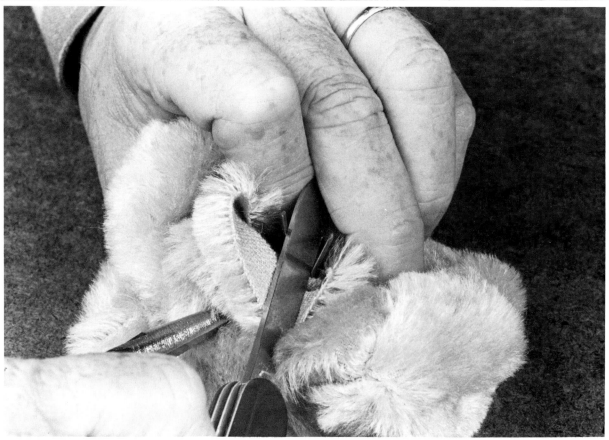

Spread the cotter pin open with a knife blade.

Bend the cotter pin away from the center, twisting into a loop.

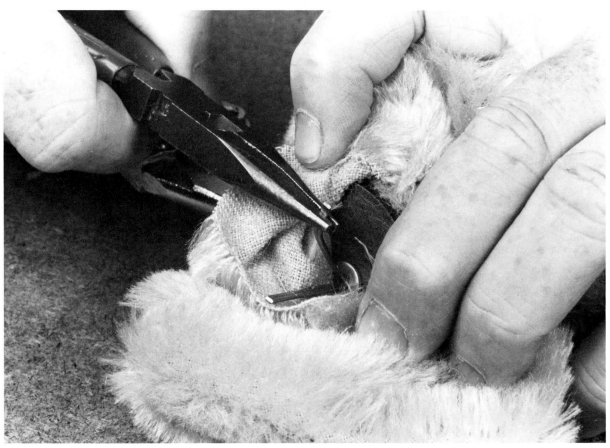

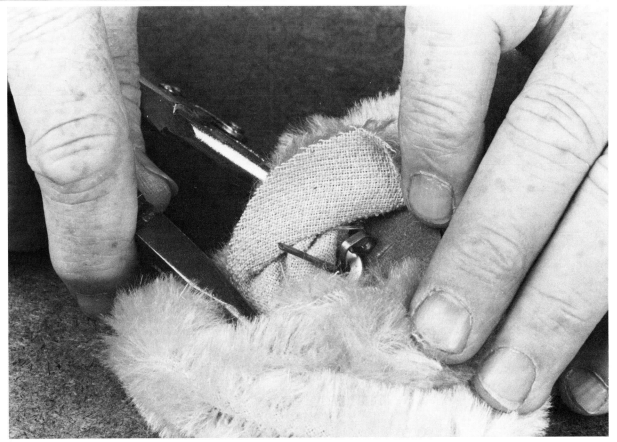

Twist it tightly into place.

Twist the other side in the opposite direction.

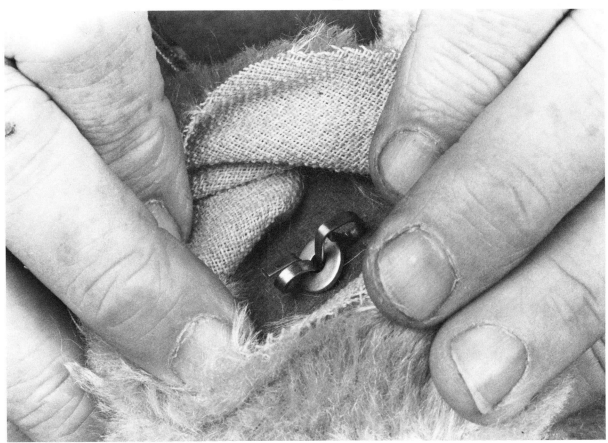

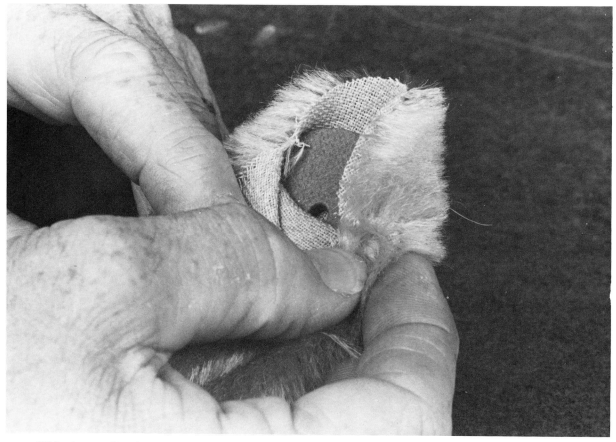

Slide the smaller disc into the arm opening, leaving ample material to sew arm opening together.

Be sure the arm seam faces the back of the bear.

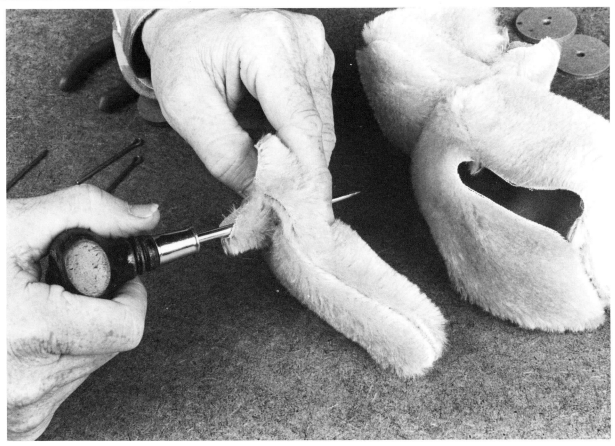

Push the scratch awl through disc and arm fabric.

After pushing scratch awl through body seam, place a second disc and align it with the first disc.

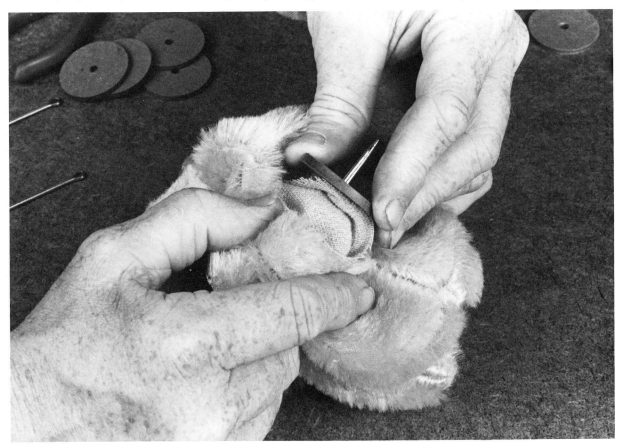

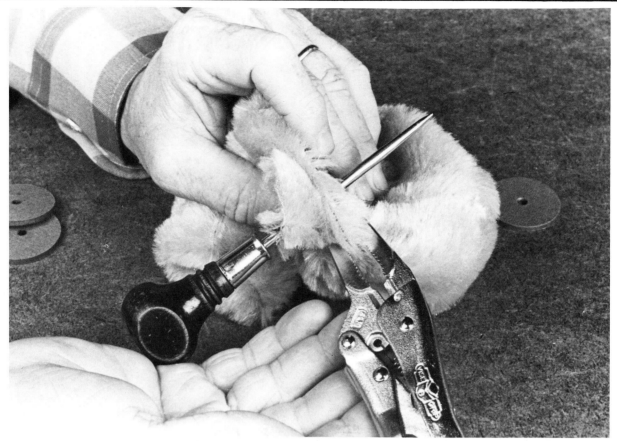

Clamp aligned discs with locking pliers.

Make sure Teddy's foot faces forward!

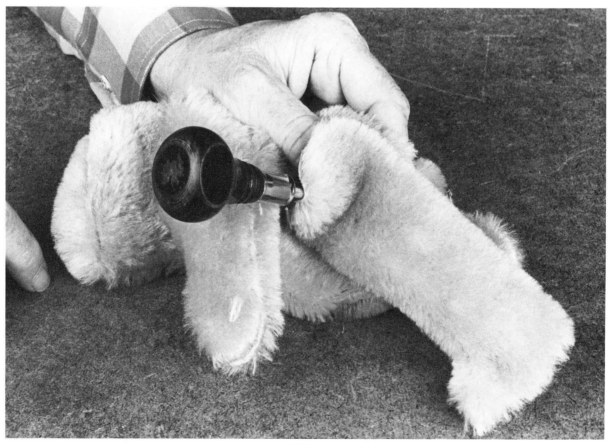

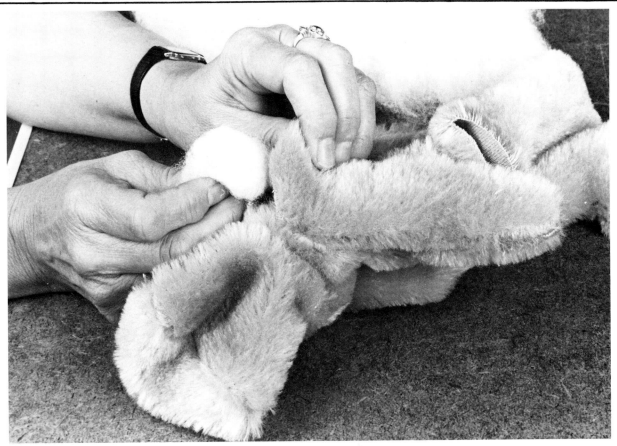

Pack the fiberfill into the bear in small pieces to avoid gaps.

A wooden spoon or dowel is a great help in packing the fiberfill.

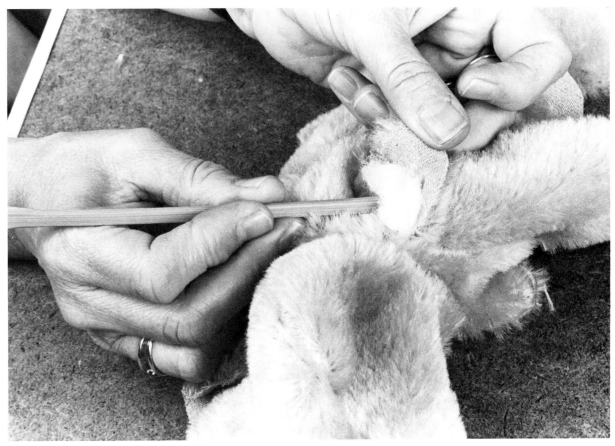

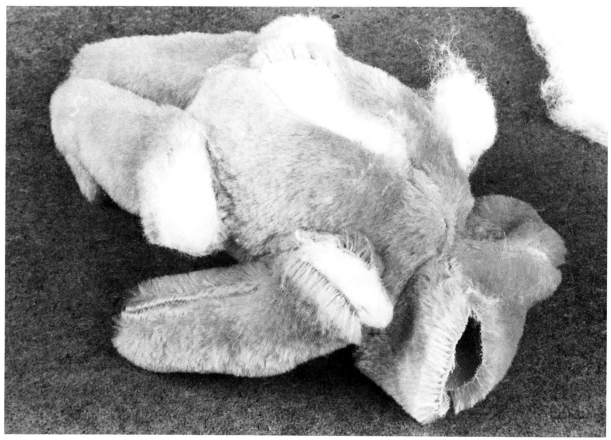

Boy, am I stuffed!

Stuff approximately one-third of the head toward the nose and bridge to allow placement of the eyes.

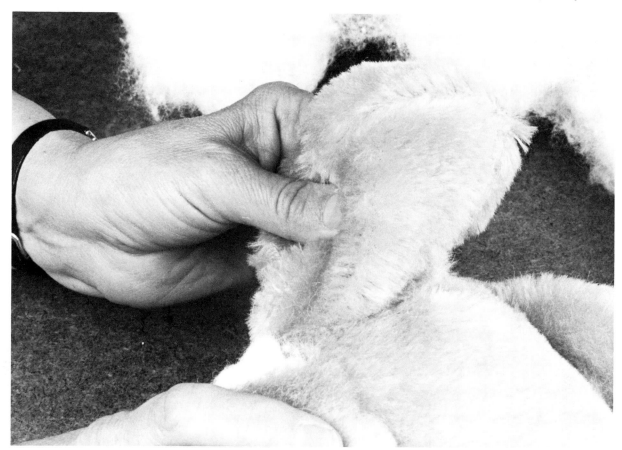

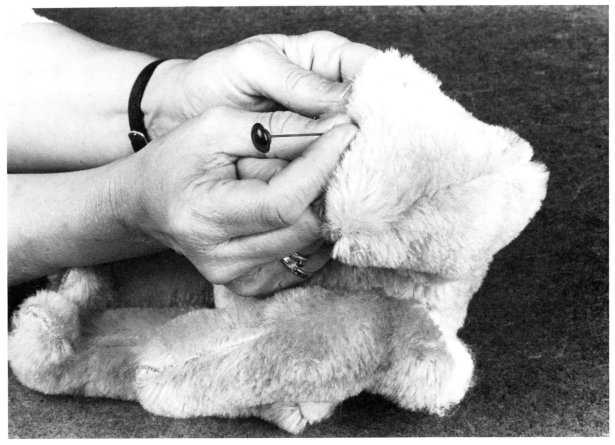

Insert each eye through the seam and through the fiberfill. Before twisting the wire in place (or the lock on plastic eyes), check to see how Teddy looks.

Try several variations for locating the eyes until he looks just right to you.

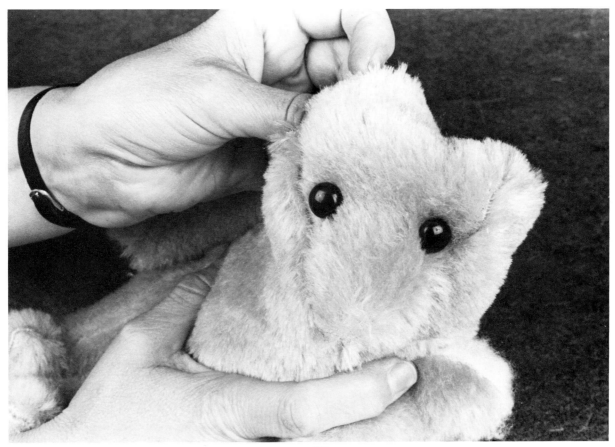

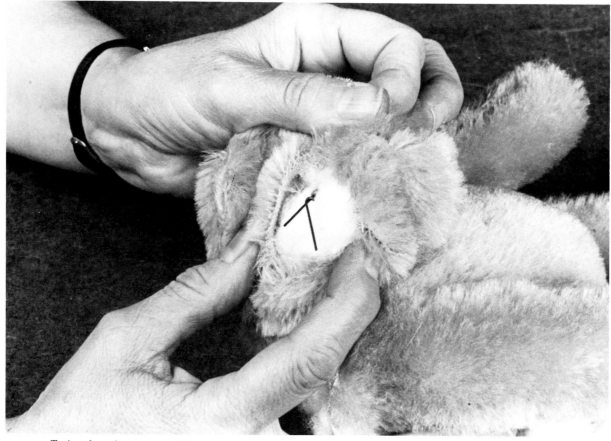

Twist the wires at least five turns; then bend the ends over so you can finish stuffing the head.

The hardboard discs can be used with cotter pins or rivets.

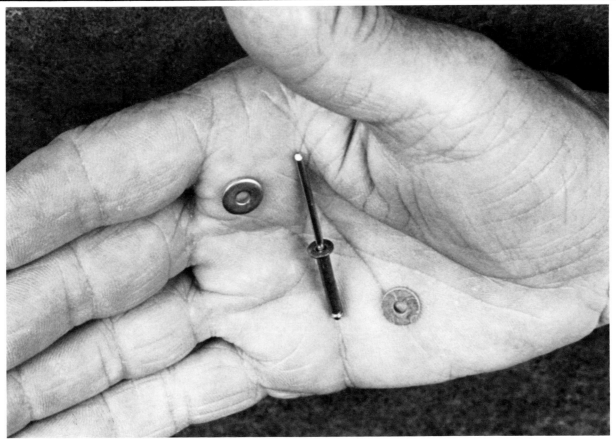

Aluminum rivet and two back-up plates (washers).

Slide a washer over the rivet shank.

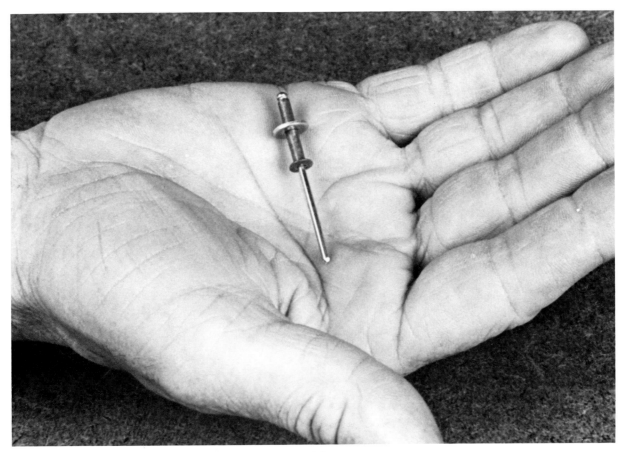

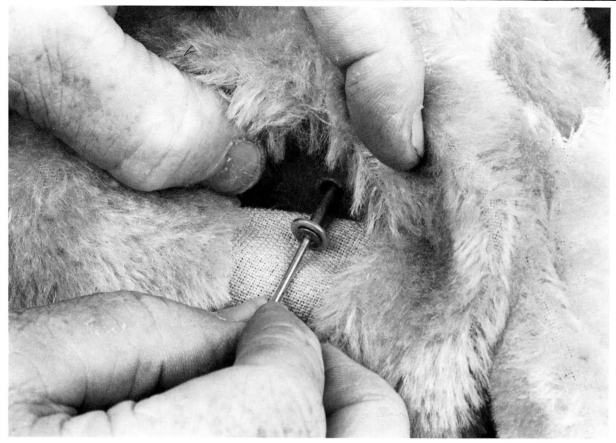

Place the rivet through the two aligned discs.

Second washer goes on opposite side of joint.

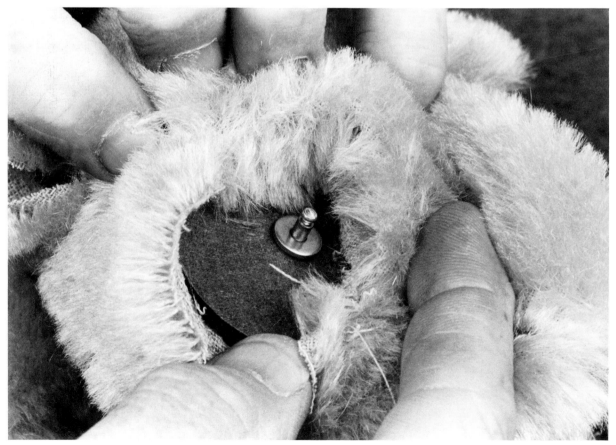

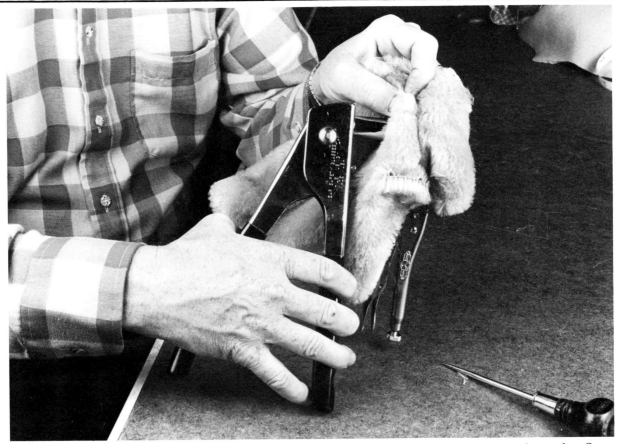

Spread the grips open on rivet gun and slide the gun nozzle over the rivet stem until it seats against the washer. Squeeze handles together. Reopen grips and slide nozzle on further. Squeeze handles again. Repeat until rivet stem "pops" or breaks loose from rivet.

Bottom side of rivet.

Top side of rivet. Note the aluminum shank has bulged out, locking the washer tightly in place.

Open the grips of the rivet gun and allow the broken stem to fall out. Discard the stem.

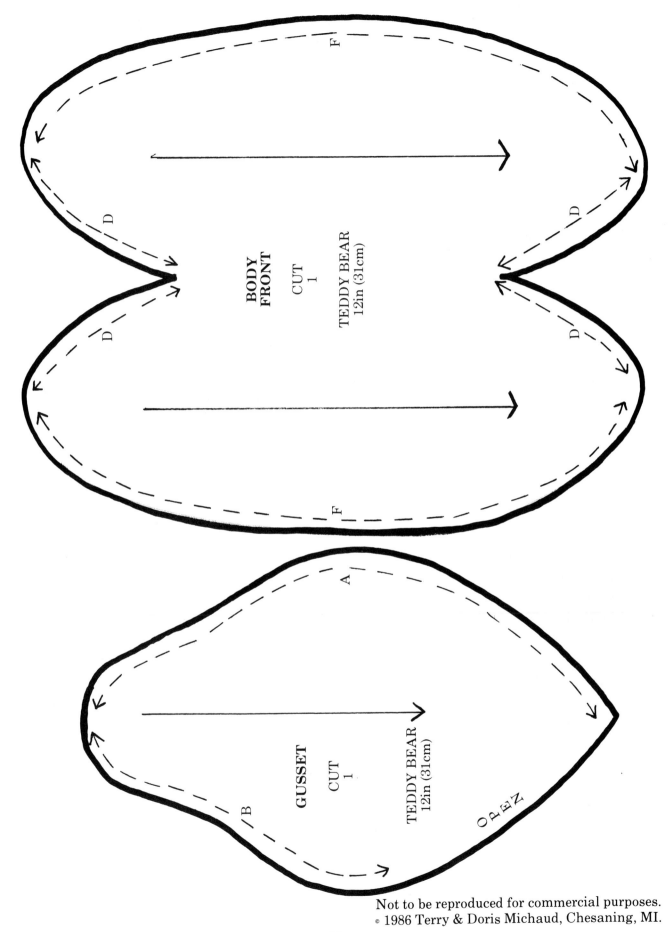

BODY
FRONT

CUT
1

TEDDY BEAR
12in (31cm)

F

D

D

D

D

F

GUSSET

CUT
1

TEDDY BEAR
12in (31cm)

A

B

OPEN

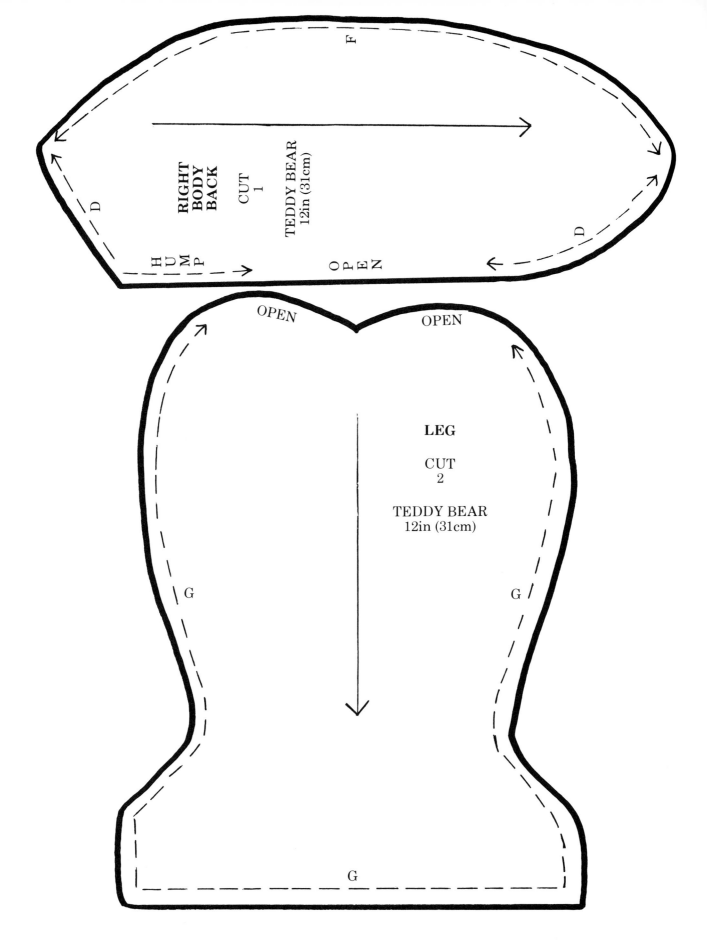

RIGHT
BODY
BACK

CUT
1

TEDDY BEAR
12in (31cm)

F

D

D

H
U
M
P

O
P
E
N

OPEN

OPEN

LEG

CUT
2

TEDDY BEAR
12in (31cm)

G

G

G

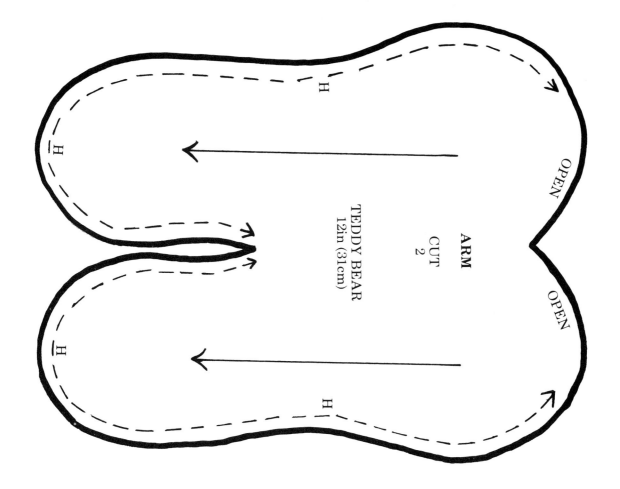

ARM
CUT
2

TEDDY BEAR
12in (31cm)

OPEN

OPEN

H

H

H

H

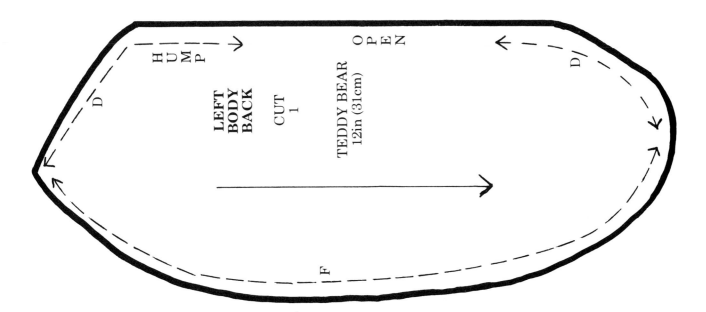

LEFT
BODY
BACK

CUT
1

TEDDY BEAR
12in (31cm)

H
U
M
P

O
P
E
N

D

D

F

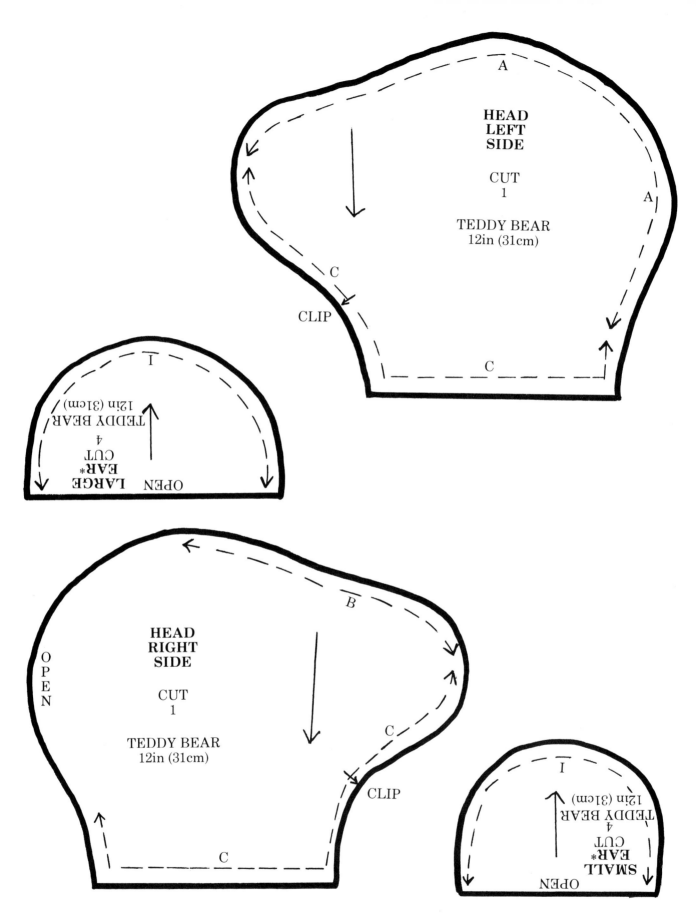

HEAD LEFT SIDE

CUT 1

TEDDY BEAR 12in (31cm)

A

A

C

CLIP

LARGE EAR*

CUT 4

TEDDY BEAR 12in (31cm)

I

OPEN

HEAD RIGHT SIDE

CUT 1

TEDDY BEAR 12in (31cm)

B

C

CLIP

C

OPEN

SMALL EAR*

CUT 4

TEDDY BEAR 12in (31cm)

I

OPEN

*A pattern for both a SMALL and a LARGE EAR are furnished. Select the one you prefer and cut 4 only of this ear for your bear.

Chapter Seven:
The Finishing Touch

We have separated this portion of the project from the first phase, because the finishing work is more demanding and can be greatly enhanced by the individual's sewing skills. It is also that talent that gives the bear its personality.

All of the seams must now be closed by hand sewing. For this procedure we will use a ladder stitch to create a nearly invisible seam. To do this, make a small running stitch 1/8 to 1/4in (.3 to .6cm) on one side of the opening; then cross over and do the same on the other side, drawing the thread snugly to close the opening.

Add stuffing and tuck in excess fabric as you go along to create a smooth and well-rounded appearance.

Close the bottom of each ear with an overcast stitch.

Pin the ears in place with a T-pin on each end. Placement is up to the discretion of the maker. Since this can dramatically alter Teddy's personality, experiment by placing the ears in a variety of locations before sewing them in place.

Start by sewing through the ear from back to front at the lower end, then through the head from front to back. Continue this stitch all the way across. Repeat for the other ear.

If you want your Teddy Bear to have the shaved muzzle shown on our mohair bear, the following procedure may be used. Since you cannot correct any errors in doing this, we recommend you experiment on a piece of scrap material before proceeding.

Using the same small scissors used for cutting the fabric, start by clipping a few hairs at a time around the end of the nose. Continue following around the nose until you have removed the plush in a circle to the base of the eyes. Do not attempt to clip too close to the backing, as a little stubble is desirable.

For Teddy's nose and mouth we use six-strand embroidery floss. Thread a needle with a large eye with all six strands, pulling it through approximately 14in (36cm). This will give you 12 strands with each pass of the needle. Leave the end knot free.

Starting 1/2in (1cm) up from the tip of the nose, pass the needle through the right seam and out the left side, pulling the end through until it just disappears. Run the needle through in the same direction, entering just below the previous hole so that the embroidery floss lays a double strand across the nose. Continue to fill the nose in until it is the desired shape.

As you make the last pass with the needle, bring it out from the center at the bottom of the nose and make a vertical stitch 1/4 to 1/2in (.6 to 1cm) long.

To form one side of the mouth, bring the needle out 3/4in (2cm) to the left, then back to the lower end of the vertical stitch.

Form the other side of the mouth in the same manner, bringing the needle in at the lower end of the vertical stitch.

Bring the needle out at the upper left hand side of the nose. Take one more stitch across and back through, bringing the needle out anywhere on the left side.

Holding the needle and embroidery floss snugly, cut it close to the fabric. The end will disappear into the stuffing.

In order to simplify our pattern, we avoided putting in foot and arm paw pads, which is one of the more difficult steps. You can create the same pad effect on the arm by shaving the front of the paw in the same manner as you create a shaved snout.

If you want your bear to have claws as we have done with ours, use the same embroidery floss and technique used on the nose. Bring the needle in through the front of the paw until the end disappears, coming out approximately 1/2in (1cm) up. After you have created three or four claws, draw the embroidery floss snugly and cut it close to the fabric so the end will disappear into the stuffing.

For the final step, use the stiff bristle brush to brush out all of the seams. Some stubborn fibers may have to be picked out with a needle, but in general the seams should brush out beautifully so they are not as pronounced.

Now that your bear has a personality, the next chapter will present some ideas on enhancing that personality with a simple bow or a complete wardrobe.

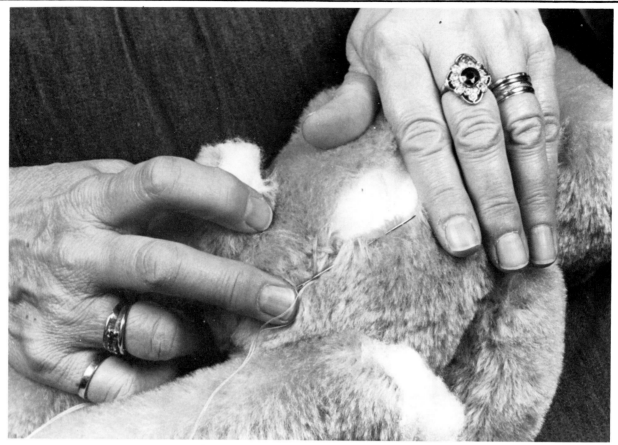

Close the openings with a running stitch.

Alternate sides with the running stitch, drawing the opening closed to make an almost invisible seam.

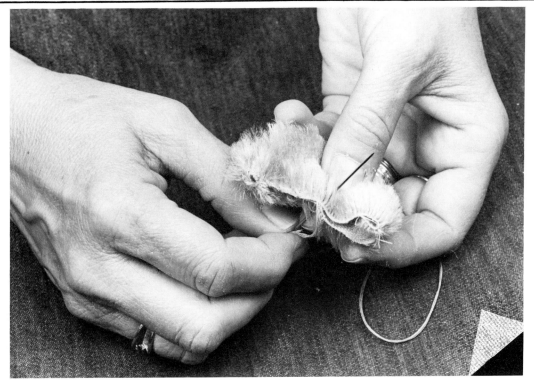

Close the bottom of each ear before pinning in place.

Pin the ears in place and check Teddy's appearance.

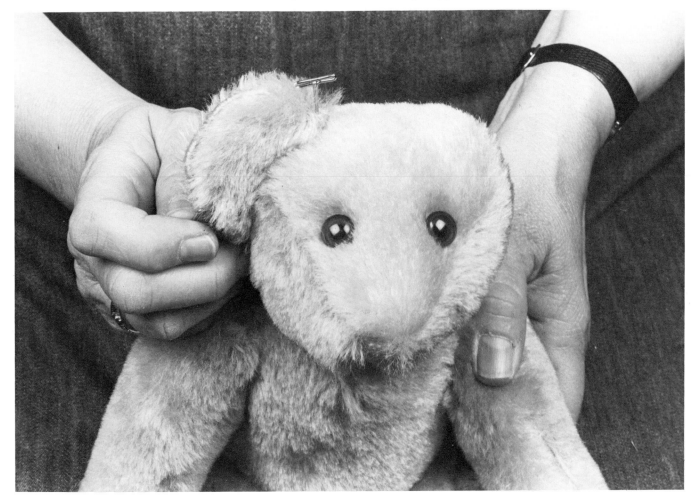

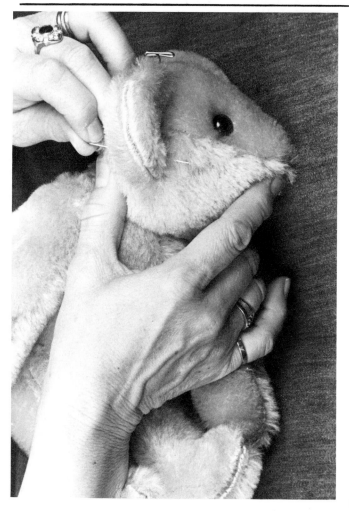

Each pass of the needle goes through the ear, then back through the head.

To trim the muzzle, start at the front of the nose with scissors. A battery operated moustache and beard trimmer may also be used.

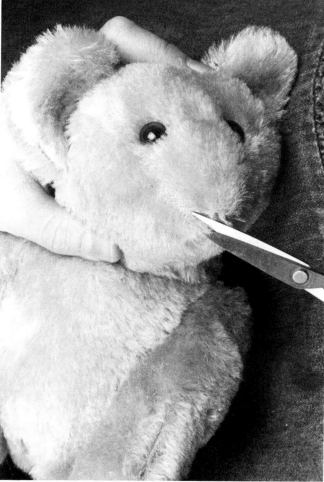

I think the barber is an ex-navy man!

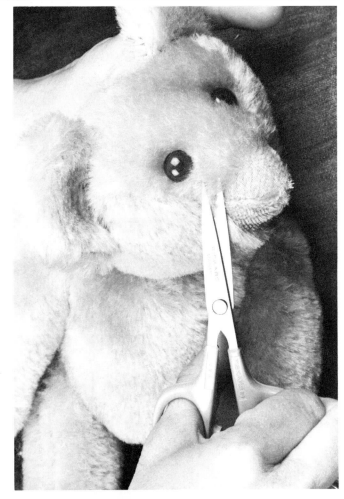

A nicely trimmed muzzle.

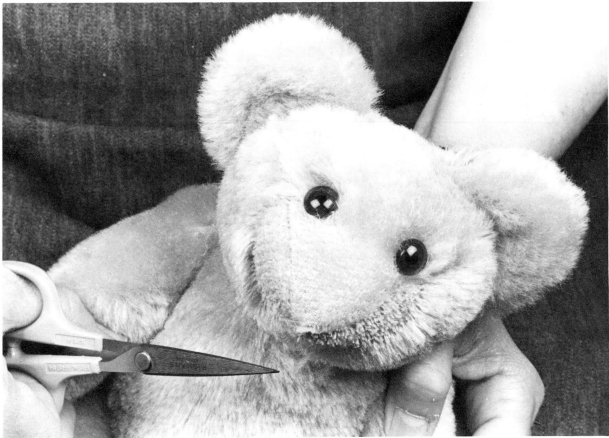

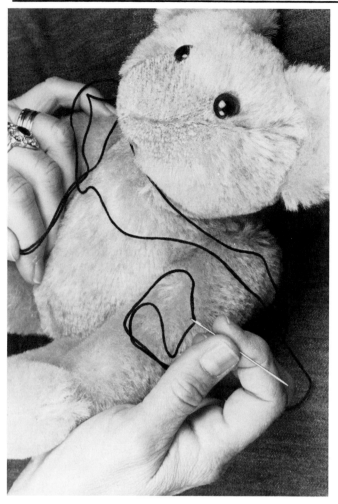

Six-strand embroidery floss doubled over makes an ideal nose and mouth.

Starting 1/3in (.8cm) up, make the first pass.

Pull the floss across the top of the nose and start the second pass.

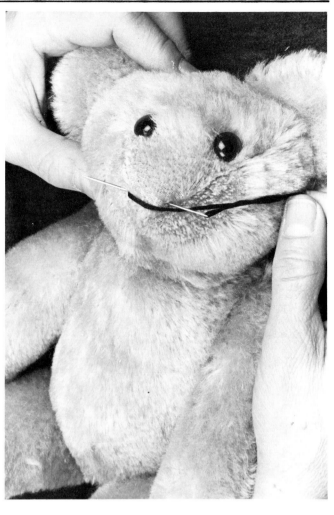

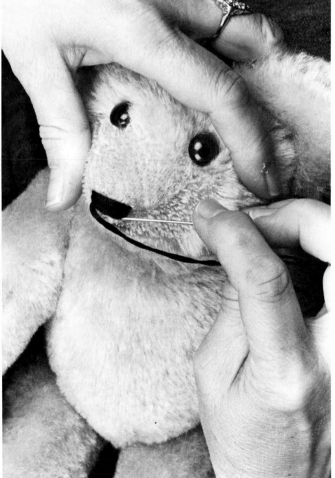

When the nose is filled in, bring the needle out at the bottom center.

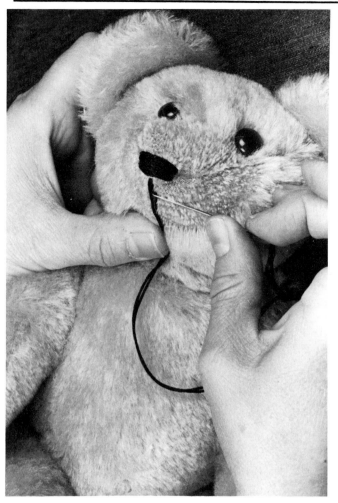

Make a vertical stitch; then start one side of the mouth.

Stitch the second side of the mouth.

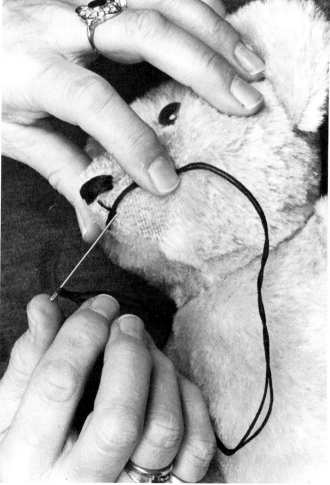

When mouth is complete, run the needle in at the center of the mouth, bringing it out at the upper left side of the nose.

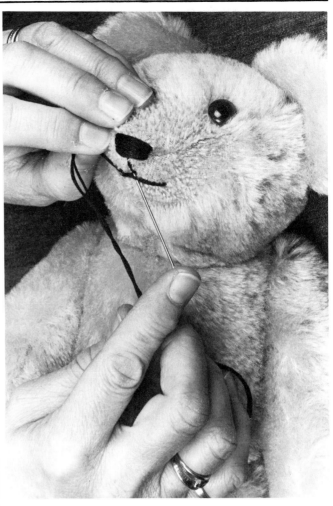

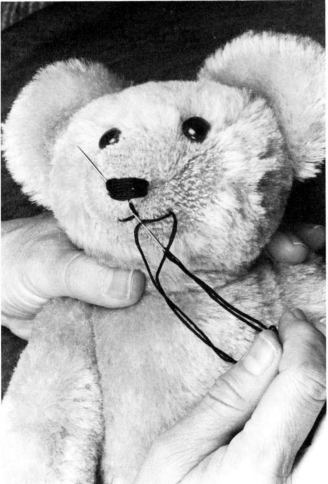

Pull the needle and embroidery floss out and make one more pass across the nose.

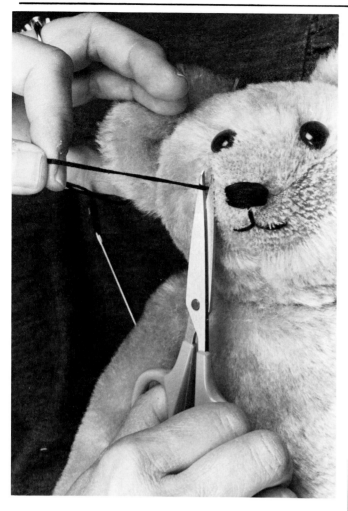

Bring the needle and floss out anywhere on the side of the nose. Draw it snug and cut it close to the fabric. The cut end will disappear inside.

To create a pad effect on the paw, trim it as you did the muzzle.

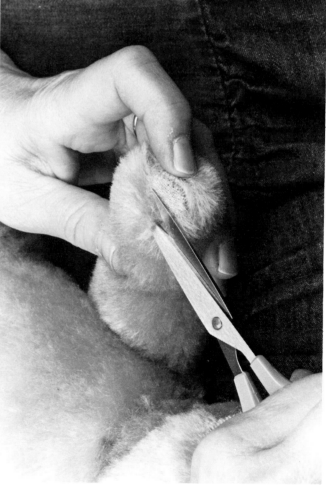

See Page 127 for additional nose and paw patterns.

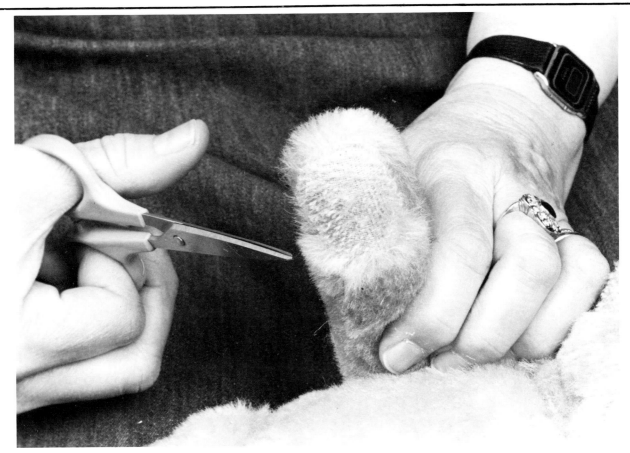

Trim a little and inspect frequently.

Claws on the paw and feet are made with the same embroidery floss used for the nose and mouth.

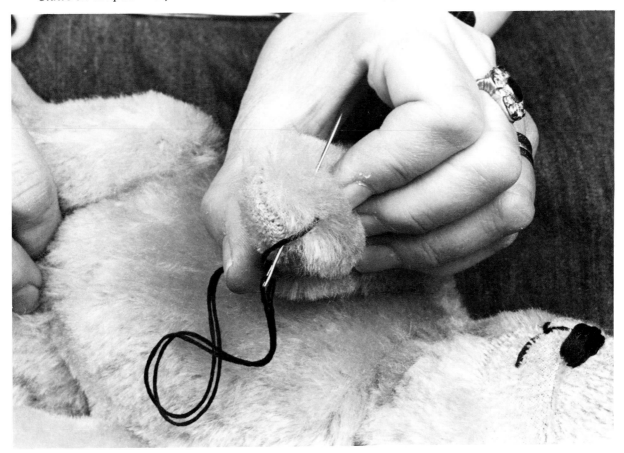

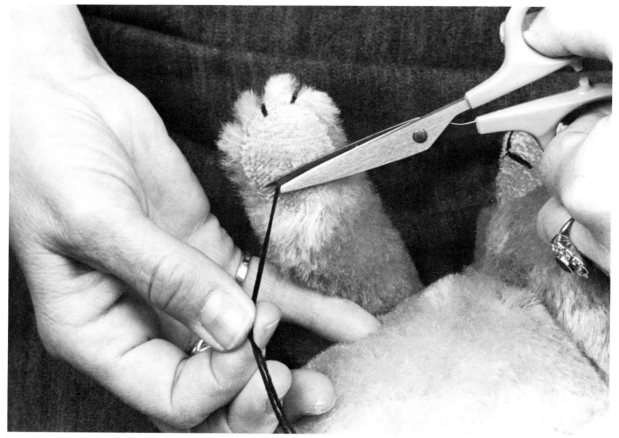

Pull the floss snug and clip close to the fabric.

Brush out the seams with a stiff bristle brush.

Chapter Eight:
Teddy's Wardrobe

If you did a survey among Teddy Bear collectors as to whether they preferred "bare" bears or costumed bears, my guess is the response would be quite evenly divided. We see a slightly higher demand for our costumed Teddies, but then we have more costumed than bare in our line. There is also a gray area in between, where a small added touch really gives the Teddy character, such as a scarf or a hat.

Dressing Teddy Bears is certainly not a new phenomenon, as some of the earliest bears came with outfits right from the factory. Our Carrousel Museum Collection of antique Teddy Bears contains many examples of this. In fact, some of the costumes were an integral part of the bear, designed so that the costume was used in place of the mohair that would normally be found underneath. After all, felt or cotton was much less expensive than mohair, even in those days.

Few Teddy Bear artists today use this substitution approach, but a large number do, in fact, use costuming as an important element in creating a special character. Teddy B and Teddy G, the Roosevelt Bears designed in plush by Donna Harrison and Dottie Ayers of Baltimore are an excellent example of the use of costuming to recreate early storybook characters, giving them added dimension. This pair of Teddies would simply be just another pair of bears without their marvelous outfits.

Peter Bull's good friend, Jack Wilson, of the House of Nisbet Ltd. in England effectively uses costuming to create a whole line of delightful Teddies in their Endangered Species series. Sally and Jim Stearns and their family produce Stearnsy Bears and Rabbits in Missouri, and they are one of the most sought after artist bears being made today. Their heartwarming bag ladies and other characters look like they have just stepped out of a Damon Runyan novel. One added touch is that they use primarily old clothing made over, or new materials distressed and stained to look old. The crowning touch is a little handwritten prose that accompanies each character.

Just as experimenting with design is appropriate, so, too, is trying a variety of approaches to adding personality to your Teddy Bear. Start with simple things, like a ribbon tied in a bow around his neck, or a scarf loosely encircling his neck and falling off to the side. Add a pair of glasses that he can peer through. Even if the glasses are too big for your size bear, it may just give him that charm you are looking for. Hats can sometimes create a special

appeal. Generally speaking, they look best cocked off to one side. An old bow tie from your husband's school days might give your bear that "Joe College" look.

Sweaters are always appropriate for Teddy Bears of all sizes. You may be fortunate to be able to crochet or have a friend that does. Doll clothes sometimes can be utilized for dressing a Teddy Bear, but most doll clothes are too tight in the neck and arms for a bear. An exception are the clothes made to fit Cabbage Patch dolls. We carry a line in our shop that are as popular with our bear collectors as they are with the Cabbage Patch doll customers.

If you are making Teddy Bears to sell, be careful not to put poor quality clothing on a top quality Teddy Bear. Let the axiom of using quality throughout be your guideline. It is most appropriate to wardrobe your handcrafted Teddy Bear in handcrafted clothing. Many artists carry their design and sewing skills right through the outfitting stage so that the entire creation is theirs. Others design appropriate costumes and "farm out" the actual sewing to others. Still others are fortunate to have access to someone who designs and makes clothing, leaving them free to concentrate their efforts on bear making. If you choose this path, you may want to check with doll collectors who can put you in touch with people who make doll clothing. Sometimes they are excited by the challenge of designing and making Teddy Bear outfits.

To keep the cost of your finished product competitive, you have to guard against getting carried away with elaborate costuming. You can often achieve the same result by using fewer pieces but going with better quality. An example of this is a Teddy Bear in our line called "Johann." Rather than going with a full outfit, we chose a pair of beautiful leather lederhosen designed and crafted by Peggy Meitmann of Bellevue, Washington. Her company is called Tailormaid Togs for Teddy Bears, and Peggy was kind enough to share the pattern for her lederhosen with the readers of *Teddy Bear and friends*® magazine in the March/April 1986 issue. We design most of our own outfits and have them handcrafted by ladies who work at home, but we were impressed with the quality and workmanship of Peggy's line so we buy this particular outfit from her.

Accessories for your Teddy Bear should be discussed in this chapter as they, too, can give your bear added appeal and charm. An old toy drum makes a perfect prop to sit your bear on, with a small tri-cornered hat for him made from folded newspaper. Small wooden and metal toys are perfect companion pieces for Teddy. Doll accessories can also be utilized, such as a doll size high chair or rocking chair. We display them in tea cups (small bears), old felt slippers, climbing into and out of wooden crates and sliding down the bannister on our stairway. Walk through the house and check out cupboards and drawers for props. You might discover a hidden treasure that will inspire an entire wardrobe for your Teddy Bear.

An early Schuco Yes/No Teddy. Felt uniform is actually part of the body. The only mohair used is on head, paws and feet.

Costuming brings two fictional Teddies to life.

House of Nisbet Ltd. artist fondly remembers an old friend.

A Stearnsy Bear finds a happy home in the Carrousel Museum collection.

My, what big eyes you have!

Sailing, sailing, over the bounding main!

112

Would you march to the beat of my drum?

Chapter Nine:
To Market, To Market

Artists and crafts persons are usually very skilled at producing a quality product, but frequently are at a loss when it comes to selling that creation. Before you can choose the marketing approach that is best suited to your needs, you must do a complete analysis of what your costs are so that you can determine a fair price for your finished work. It seems simple enough at first glance. Take the cost of a little fabric and thread and add a little for your time. Unfortunately, this is the approach taken by all too many talented producers. Worse yet, some feel their time is not worth much because, "I really wasn't doing anything anyway."

In order to determine a fair price for that marvelous little Teddy Bear you have just created, you have to be honest with yourself. Obviously, your end goal plays an important part here. If your project is directed toward making several bears along with other friends for a church bazaar, then you can, indeed, eliminate a cost for your time as it makes more profit for the church. If you hope to build a business that will provide you with a profitable return, then everything associated with the project is important.

Take a pad and pencil and make a list of the materials involved. Take the price of your fabric and divide by the number of Teddies you get out of a yard and you have your fabric cost. How much thread goes into your bear? There is a temptation to write off some of the incidentals that only cost pennies but remember we want to come up with an honest cost figure, so everything has to be included. How about the pad material? It is just a few cents but it is a cost. Embroidery thread for the nose and mouth goes on the list as well. If your bear is jointed, include the hardboard discs that your husband cut for you, and do not forget his time as well, which will be included with labor costs later in the list. He may have cut those discs from a piece of scrap material he had lying around but if you reach a point where he runs out of scrap and has to buy material, it is important to include the cost. Holding the joints together with washers and cotter pins? Write it down. Include the cost of stuffing materials. What about the bow around Teddy's neck? True, it came out of your ribbon box, but sooner or later it has to be replaced. Sew-in labels or hang tags go on the list.

Running a total gives us our primary materials cost. Now we put down our labor cost, which will require an accurate time study. You need to include all the time spent, from cutting the fabric, sewing the parts, putting in the joints (do not forget your husband's time cutting them), stuffing your bear, sewing the ears on and the time-consuming finishing work. Only a minute to put the bow on? That is 1/60th of an hour and should be included.

After completing the basic materials and labor cost, many artists feel they have determined the cost and can, therefore, come up with a selling cost. However, for this cost picture to be accurate, we now have to look at some of the hidden costs. This is particularly important if you discover your Teddy is a big hit and orders start rolling in. We have talked with a number of artists in this situation. They have a ton of orders on the books and have come to the realization that they are not making any money after all their hard work. Frustration sets in and they finally give up in disgust.

Packaging is a cost that is frequently overlooked. The bear does not necessarily have to go in a gift box, but he has to get from you to the customer somehow. Whether it is in a bag or a box, it is a cost of doing business. This is particularly important if you are doing mail order business. Packing tissue around him? Write it down. Do not forget the packaging tape!

How about advertising? How do you plan to let the world know about your wonderful product? Whether it is a classified ad, a mailing to a collector list or a full-page ad in *Teddy Bear and friends®* magazine, it has to be a factor in your cost figures. It can be difficult to break down your advertising costs per bear, but make some sort of projection for a given time period; then divide that by the number of bears you will produce in the same time frame. The cost of doing a Teddy Bear or doll show is included under advertising and promotion.

Now that we have covered the out-of-pocket expenses, we are ready to look at the one factor that can make the difference between profit and loss, particularly as your business grows. That factor is time. Time, time, time. It takes time to take care of correspondence. If you are dealing with over 100 accounts in 37 states, it can be a significant amount of time taking care of correspondence and phone messages. It takes time to package your product once you have completed it. It takes time to prepare advertising. Even if you had extra help with some of these chores, it takes someone's time, and you must look ahead to the point where you have to hire extra help to take care of these things.

This listing we have discussed may, indeed, not be all inclusive but it makes the point that if you do not recognize your true cost of making the Teddy

Bear, you may end up with no profit for your effort.

The final item that goes on the list is profit. If you are satisfied that your time has been adequately compensated for under your labor cost, then you have completed your task. If you are building a business, however, you will not succeed without a profit. Keep in mind that this represents a gross profit. Your bookkeeper will add all other costs of doing business (heat, lights, rent and so forth) to determine your net profit for tax purposes. The percentage of profit you need to add will be largely determined by the marketing method you choose. Some of those figures will be discussed in the following chapters.

The choice of how to sell your Teddy Bear requires a careful examination of your situation, needs and desires. How many Teddies can you produce in a year? Some of the artists we know work full time jobs and can only devote a small amount of time to their hobby. It is not in their best interest to take a lot of orders from retailers that they cannot possibly fill. In this situation, one can sell at shows or by mail. How much help do you have to develop a business? Our business is a full-time endeavor at this point and we each average from 12 to 14 hours a day, seven days a week. If you are serious about building a full-time business, it requires this kind of effort to succeed. If you are unable or unwilling to make that kind of sacrifice, then that should be a major factor in the marketing method you select.

The many variations of sales avenues open to you are discussed in the following two chapters. But before making any decisions on which method suits your needs, it would be prudent to test market your completed bear. Attend a few shows and see what others are making and selling. Notice I said selling, not just offering. Sometimes you can learn as much by waiting until the end of the show to see what did not sell, which may have been due to poor craftsmanship, overpricing or both. If you are convinced you have a top quality product and your price is fair (to you as well as the buyer), then book a show and see what the public thinks. A Teddy Bear show would be preferable, but if there is not one in your area, find a doll show, or an arts and crafts market. Even if selling at shows is not your ultimate goal, it can provide needed exposure and feedback with minimum risk or investment. Talk to other bear makers as well. See what success they have experienced. Sometimes choosing the right show can make a huge difference, and sometimes it is as unpredictable as the weather. We have booked shows where we had only moderate success one year and returned the second year to do an outstanding show. What works for one person may not work for another. That is why it is vitally important to tailor your program to your needs.

ITEM	COST
PLUSH FABRIC	4.50
PAD FABRIC	.16
THREAD	.25
EYES	2.95
GROWLER	2.00
EMBROIDERY THREAD	.25
FIBREFILL	3.00
10 HARDBOARD JOINTS	1.50
5 COTTER PINS	.50
PINK RIBBON	1.00
SEW-IN LABEL	.65
	$ 16.76

Make an accurate list of all materials.

LABOR COST

TASK	TIME
CUT FABRIC	30 MINUTES
SEW PARTS	40
JOIN BEAR	20
STUFF BEAR	20
PUT IN EYES	15
HAND SEWING	45
SEW NOSE	20
SEW EARS	20
	3 1/2 HOURS

TOTAL TIME × HOURLY RATE = LABOR COST

Since time is the key factor, make a complete accounting.

ADDITIONAL MATERIALS

ITEM	COST
HANG TAG	.18
PAPER BAG	.06
SHIPPING BOX	1.25
TISSUE	.05
PACKAGING TAPE	.12
ADVERTISING	2.25
SHIPPING	3.10
	$7.01

The items most often overlooked.

ADDITIONAL LABOR

TASK	TIME
PACKAGING	10 MINUTES
CORRESPONDENCE	5
PREPARE ADVERTISING	2
DESIGN WORK	8
	25 MINUTES

Time is the artist's most precious commodity.

Chapter Ten:
Selling To The Consumer

Probably the most popular selling method chosen by most bear makers is selling directly to the collector. One reason for this is the direct contact the maker has with the buyer. Most artists and crafts people enjoy the positive response to their creation from the buyer. Most collectors look forward to meeting the creator of the Teddy they are buying, so it becomes a mutual admiration society. Let's face it; most of us love to be loved, and the admiration expressed about our work goes a long way toward driving us during the long hours of creating the finished product.

Another reason many makers choose the direct sale route is the pricing does not have to include a dealer's profit and can, therefore, be priced lower. If you can sell all the product you can make directly to the collector, this is very likely the path for you to choose.

There are actually three separate and distinct marketing routes to go in selling direct. The one many artists prefer is selling at shows. Here, again, you have the opportunity of meeting the buyer of your product face to face and getting that all-important feedback. There is a great deal of flexibility in this sales method in that you can work at your own pace, then book shows when and where you want to. It will, in most cases, require a minimum amount of travel, depending on your geographic location. If you live in California, shows can be a way of life. Most shows are reasonable for booth space, and it also affords you the opportunity of seeing what other makers are offering the public and at what price. It also gives you an opportunity to shop for bear making supplies.

Mail order is another option open to the bear maker. In fact, if your location is remote, it may be the only logical plan for you. One of the negative aspects of selling by mail is the desire by some collectors to see the product. We deal with this by offering a 10-day return privilege. I have questioned others who sell by mail and they feel that this is not a major obstacle. Selling by mail will require an expenditure for advertising. It can be an elaborate display ad in *Teddy Bear and friends*® magazine or some other publication that reaches the bear collector. Or, it can be an inexpensive classified ad in one of these publications. Whatever method of advertising you choose, plan to run the ad for several consecutive issues. Readers often have to see an ad several times before they respond.

A mailing list can be a valuable asset in building a mail order business but it can take years to acquire a good list. You can also rent lists; however, be sure to check the validity of such a list. You can produce a simple mailer, a color brochure or a catalog. This is an approach that calls for some measure of experience, as it can be extremely expensive to produce even a simple color folder. We request the person inquiring send a self-addressed stamped envelope and $1.00 to offset this cost.

The third option in selling directly to the collector is to open a retail shop. It can be as simple as a room in your home or a retail space in a shopping center. If a larger store is your goal, you may want to handle other handcrafted and manufactured Teddy Bears as well as your own, and perhaps handle other collector items. Needless to say, this approach is going to require a substantial investment in time and money. Even the small one-room shop in your home will require city permits, assuming you are in a location where it is permitted at all.

If you are attracted to the idea of having a shop, you need to first determine if you have a large enough population to support such a store. Are there other shops of this type in your area and are they successful? Another consideration is the need to maintain somewhat regular shop hours. You must recognize going into this project that you will be tying yourself down. If you do weigh all the pros and cons and decide in favor of a retail store, start small and grow. One big factor in your rate of growth will be the ability to plow back all the profits into the store without taking anything out. This means you will need some other means of support. A working husband or winning the state lottery can help!

Many successful craft marketers actually use a combination of these selling methods. There is a growing number of bear makers who sell at shows and sell by mail as well. They take advantage of the opportunity at shows to build a mailing list of names of collectors at the show, then do follow-up mailings to them. Some entrepreneurs just record the names and addresses of those who make purchases, and some put out a registry book and ask everyone to sign it.

Many shop owners take advantage of the added market exposure they get by doing shows outside their immediate area. It not only introduces their line to new collectors, but it affords them the opportunity to discover and obtain new lines for their shop. The more aggressive among us not only employ all of these methods, but we wholesale as well! Perhaps that is why we find ourselves working day and night, seven days a week.

We asked some of our collector friends how they felt about handcrafted Teddy Bears. Susan Allis of East Lansing, Michigan, prefers handcrafted bears to the mass produced variety. She says, "I like to feel my bear was very special to its maker, not done by many hands in an assembly line." Susan looks for quality of design which, of course, includes uniqueness at affordable prices. Marilyn Risch of West Chicago, Illinois, loves artist bears because they are made with love and care and, therefore, have an individual personality. She also looks for quality of materials and uniqueness. She loves the added personal touch of the artist or maker.

Uniqueness, caring and love is what Sig and Sandy Humanski of Toledo, Ohio, find in the handcrafted Teddies in their collection. They say there is always room for another unique bear in their family. They lean toward the "undressed" Teddies but if the costume somehow enhances the personality of the bear, he will find a welcome spot in their home. They had this word of advice to the bear maker. "When making a bear, the primary concern should be creating a winning, charming personality. If life has been 'breathed' into a Teddy in terms of a special personality, he (or she) will have no problem finding a good home and a loving owner."

Margaret J. Lee of Dearborn, Michigan, has an outstanding collection that she frequently shares with the public on television and in talks around the state. Margaret, known in bear circles as "The Bearoness," prefers originality and quality, and feels that artist bears are folk art. Her message to the bear maker is to "be original and true to your ideal. Use good materials and put them together with care. The bear market is crowded, but really fine bears sell well, and fine reproductions of antique

bears are sought after because we (collectors) can't have the originals." Jack McCutchan of Lebanon, Indiana, is another collector who likes the better quality and imagination shown in the handcrafted Teddies. He likes the 10 to 21in (25 to 53cm) size range, priced from $50. to $150.

Paul and Rosemary Volpp of California have one of the finest collections of antique and contemporary Teddy Bears in the country. They are a popular duo on the lecture circuit and frequently do feature articles in *Teddy Bear and friends*® magazine on decorating for holidays and special events with Teddy Bears. They are attracted to the artist bears because "they are generally better made and have that special appeal of being more limited in numbers." They, like the other collectors we talked with, are drawn to uniqueness of design. Rosemary says, "One of my all time favorites is Carrousel's Uncle Sam (our Limited Edition of a few years ago) because he embodies all our requirements...quality for a reasonable price, theme and so on."

Remember that very first Carrousel Teddy Bear we talked about at the beginning of the book? When Sir Edward II arrived in Boston and the shop owner called to place an order, he had a word of advice that has remained as a guideline in every bear we make. He said, "It is obvious you have taken a lot of time to create a top quality, unique Teddy Bear. But after you went to all that time and trouble, you topped him off with a cheap ribbon! If you are going to make a quality product, make it quality all the way through." His constructive criticism was well-founded, and we have taken heed to his advice ever since. Strive for originality and quality at a fair price, and there will always be a demand for your work.

Teddy Bear and friends® *magazine has a column to advertise your product.*

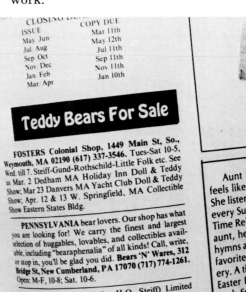

119

Flyers and brochures are ideal for a mail order promotion.

You may want to develop a computerized mailing list.

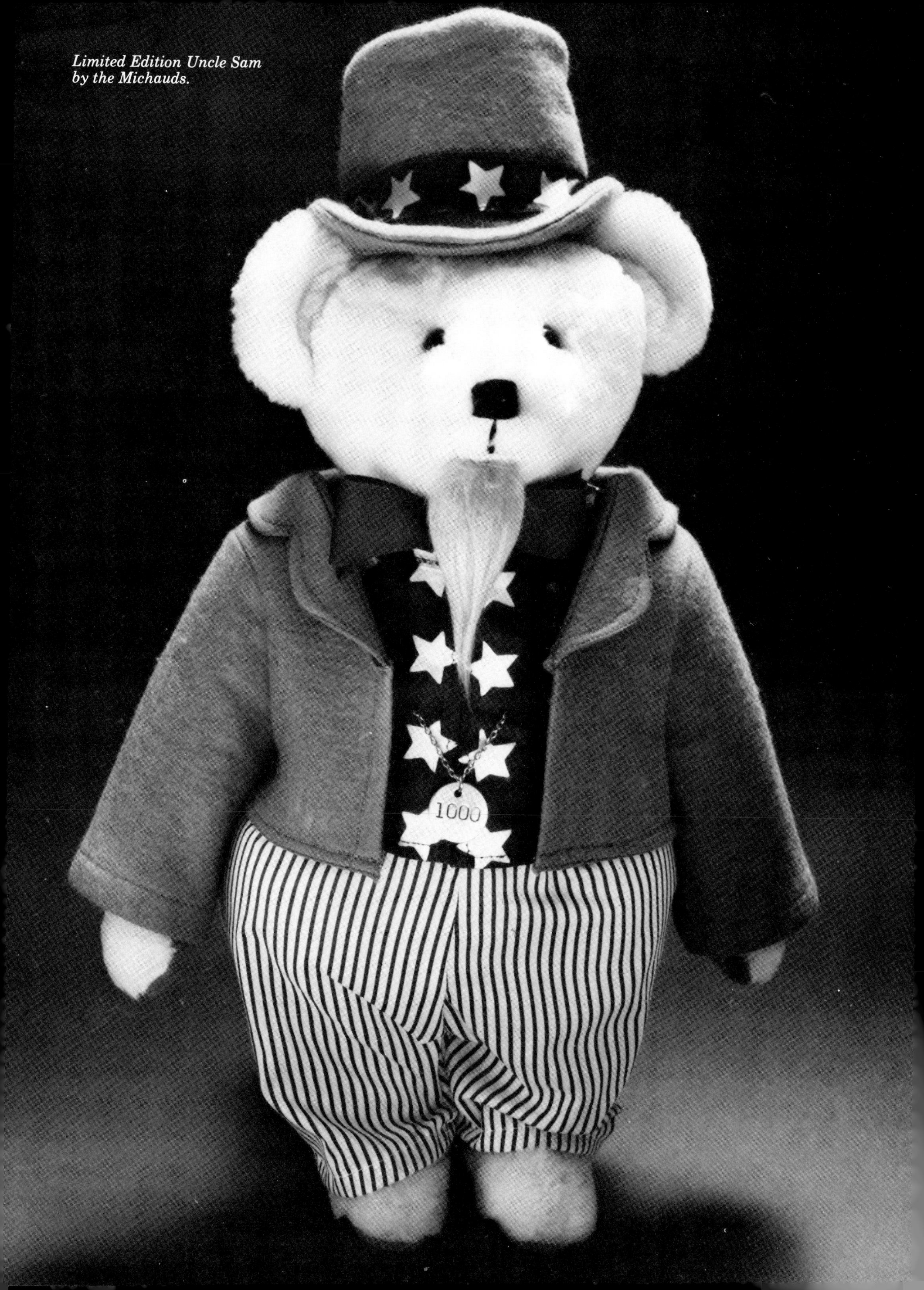

Limited Edition Uncle Sam by the Michauds.

Sir Edward II, ready to find a new home.

Chapter Eleven:
Selling To The Retailer

Let us make the assumption that you can produce more Teddy Bears than you have the time or desire to sell yourself. Or, your forte is the artistic creation, not the marketing end of the business. You may prefer to stay home and create and avoid the public altogether. If you find yourself in this situation, or you want to expand on your sales opportunities beyond doing shows and/or mail order, but still have no desire to open your own shop, you should investigate selling your wares to a retail shop.

To be comfortable in dealing with a shop owner, you need to understand some basics of the retail business. One artist who looked into this marketing approach was horrified to find out that the Teddy Bear she sold to the shop owner was going to be sold at a 50 percent profit margin to the dealer. "Why, that shop will make more from my work than I will!" was her unhappy conclusion. Being involved in all aspects of the business gives us the position of seeing both sides of the coin. It does appear at first glance that the retailer is being somewhat unrealistic in his markup, but when you analyze what his costs are, it becomes most reasonable. That shop owner has a lot of expenses that have to come out of his share of the profits from the sale of your Teddy Bear. Every morning when he opens his door, he has a host of fixed expenses whether he makes a sale that day or not. He has rent to pay, an electrical bill, sales clerks to pay, advertising to sell your bear (more than a modest expense in most cases), packaging to pay for (even a new paper bag costs money), insurance costs, shoplifting losses, and more often than not the need to sell some merchandise at a loss because it became dirty and shopworn from handling, or it just plain did not sell! I have not even scratched the surface on additional costs faced by most shop owners, but I think it may help you to understand his position. Do not forget, if you choose to sell directly to the consumer, you, too, will be faced with many of these costs.

Another factor comes into play here, in that the largest mistake made by many artists and crafters is underpricing their work. More often than not it is based on the burning desire to sell, sell, sell. The assumption is made that if I make my prices lower, more people will want it. That may not be totally true. If your work is of poor quality, your choice of materials is based on the lowest cost, your work is not original, or a combination of these things, then the price you are asking may be too high no matter how low it is. Frequently we base the price on what we or some friend or relative is willing to pay. When

an associate (who is not a Teddy Bear collector) first saw one of our bears, he said, "They're beautiful, but I'd never pay that much for a Teddy Bear!" My response was that I probably would not either, but we were really making them for people who not only would, but did. He walked away laughing, with perhaps a little better understanding of marketing. If you do not believe you are dealing with a widely diversified market, just look at the price range of "factory made" Teddy Bears that are sold day in and day out. You will find them from a few dollars to a few hundred dollars. Obviously, the producer whose goods are commanding prices of several hundred dollars does not expect to capture the same market volume that the $5 Teddy Bear will reach, based on total number of bears produced. Our $150. Professor is not likely taking business away from the $13. Smokey Bear produced by R. Dakin & Company.

The conclusion that can be drawn is that there is, indeed, a market for your product no matter where you price it, within reason. If you price at the high end, you have a narrow market, but that market share in numbers may still be more than you can produce. This is not meant to encourage over pricing, but to perhaps demonstrate that by realistic pricing, you may still have enough margin to sell on a wholesale basis so that you and the shop owner make a reasonable profit.

Some shops will take your product on consignment, which means you get paid when the product gets sold. Usually you will make a better margin of profit per Teddy Bear, but you may have your money tied up for long periods of time. Very few bear makers we have talked with take this approach. You may be surprised to know that most shop owners prefer outright purchase. Mickie Veale who owns and operates Creekwood Bear Company in Houston rarely takes a consignment arrangement. Her recommendation to the bear maker is "to create your own pattern with a totally unique expression. Collectors are smart enough to recognize a bear that has been made from a purchased pattern." Regarding price, Mickie says, "Everyone likes a bargain, but if you have a top of the line expensive bear, people recognize quality and don't mind paying for it." She feels that Teddy Bears in the 8 to 12in (20 to 31cm) size sell best in the price range of $45. to $95. retail.

Donna Harrison and Dottie Ayers of the Calico Teddy in Baltimore also avoid consignment merchandise because of the added book work. They advise the artist or bear maker to extend 30 day terms to the retailer (almost all merchandise purchased by shop owners is purchased on this basis). The Teddies should always have sewn on tags and card tags to identify and number. They should also have a ribbon or something to give the bear character. Jane Servinski of Maple Hill Nursery and Doll Shoppe in Midland, Michigan, agrees that top quality artists bears sell better to her collectors. She boils it down to three words: "Good workmanship sells."

Beth Savino and her family operate Hobby Center Toys stores throughout several midwestern states. Beth looks for quality first when she is buying for her shops, then decides if the price is appropriate. She says that they are always looking for the unusual in Teddy Bears, and she emphasizes that the quality must extend to not only the Teddy, but also his wardrobe.

Now that we have cautioned the reader about underpricing your work, a word of warning about overpricing comes from Joan Venturino of Bears To Go in Berkeley, California. Joan is a pioneer in the Teddy Bear specialty store business and now operates two specialty stores and a thriving mail order business as well. Joan warns the promising artist that your price has to be realistic. This supports our recommendation that you attend shows and see what is selling. Joan does use consignment with new artists until she determines that the work will sell in her shop. Sometimes the Teddy does not fit in with her product mix. If it does sell, she then purchases outright. Joan also supports the feeling of other shop owners that original design is most important.

It would be wrong to draw the conclusion that all retailers sell only high-priced merchandise. Some shops are designed to cater to just adult collectors, while others have full selection toy and doll shops and offer a wide price range. This supports the theory that there is a market out there for Teddies in a host of price ranges. It is merely a question of finding your niche in that market.

If you do not value your work, no one else will.

If you over value your work, you may not have to worry about meeting the demand.

Chapter Twelve:

Conclusions

In this book we have attempted to share our experiences and some excellent advice from some of the bear makers and artists, collectors and shop owners it has been our privilege to work with over the years. We feel it would be appropriate to summarize some of the primary considerations for the novice and the experienced bear maker alike.

1. Once you have created an acceptable pattern, make the bear in a variety of materials, as they all appear dramatically different.
2. Buy fabric and other supplies in small quantity until you are certain they will do the jobs you intend them to do.
3. Experiment with your designs. Be daring. Be different.
4. Do an accurate forecast of your costs, but be realistic in your final price.
5. Talk to other bear makers and collectors to understand their feelings.
6. If you wholesale your product to a retailer, recognize that the shop owner is working hard to enhance your reputation. Do not damage his by underselling him.
7. Be honest in your commitments and follow through with promises.
8. Share your experience and knowledge with others to upgrade the whole Teddy Bear making process, whether it be your vocation or avocation.
9. Be original! Collectors know a copy when they see one.
10. Strive for quality workmanship using quality materials. It will outsell even low-priced poor quality.
11. The final judge of your creativity and workmanship is the collector. Respect their judgement, for without them we are nothing.

Important Addresses

Carrousel (The Michaud Collection)
505 W. Broad St.
Chesaning, MI 48616
Phone (517) 845-7881
Fax (517) 845-6650

Authors' address. Holds periodic workshops in various locations.

Good Bears of the World
P.O. Box 13097
Toledo, OH 43613
Phone & Fax: (419) 531-5365

This charitable organization has dens all over the world. They provide free teddy bears to children in hospitals and to senior citizens. Quarterly magazine.

Teddy Bear & friends® Magazine
Cowles Magazine Inc.
6405 Flank Drive
Harrisburg, PA 17112
1-800-435-9610

Magazine published 6 times per year.

Teddy Bear Review
Collector Communications Corp.
170 Fifth Avenue
New York, NY 10010
1-800-347-6969

Magazine published 6 times per year.

Hobby House Press, Inc.
1 Corporate Drive
Grantsville, MD 21536
1-800-554-1447

Publisher of a wide range of books related to teddy bear and doll collecting, making, etc.

REGISTER OF COPYRIGHTS
Library of Congress
Washington, DC 20559